ARCHITECTURE NOW!
VOL. 10

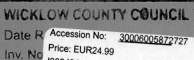

ARCHI TEC TURE NOW!

PHILIP JODIDIO

VOL. 10

TASCHEN

44

50

74

78

108

114

150

CULTURE & RELIGION

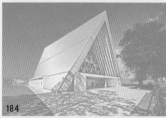

190

196

246

LEISURE

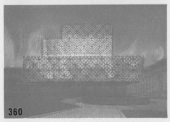

CONTENTS

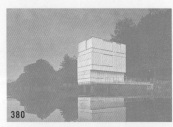

EDUCATION & RESEARCH

INTRODUCTION

ROMANCING THE STONE

In its 10th edition, the *Architecture Now!* series of books has taken an indisputable place in the world of buildings on paper. When the first *Architecture Now!* volume was published in 2001, figures who still mark the profession were already present: Tadao Ando, Zaha Hadid, Herzog & de Meuron, Fumihiko Maki, Richard Meier, Morphosis, Christian de Portzamparc, Álvaro Siza, and Eduardo Souto de Moura, to name only the past and future Pritzker Prize winners, were all there. So were many others who have since gone on to take a significant place in international circles. Published in at least six languages, distributed worldwide, *Architecture Now!* has done a great deal to "popularize" a form of creativity often marked by a more closed attitude. With texts and images that can be understood by non-specialists, the series seeks to nonetheless be fully accurate and reliable, qualities frequently lacking in the huge numbers of magazine articles and books about architecture for the general public that have circulated in the past 13 years. Each entry in these books is submitted to the architects to insure accuracy, but the choice of projects published, the texts, and indeed the selection of illustrations are the work of the author/editor given responsibility for the series from the outset by the publisher.

ON THE EDGE OF SENSORY DEPRIVATION

Architectural criticism has been durably marked by works such as the 1932 classic *The International Style* by Philip Johnson and Henry-Russell Hitchcock, or the numerous volumes by Charles Jencks on postmodernism. If it wasn't "post" then it had to be newer than that and, above all, architecture had to be neatly packaged into the zeitgeist, ever so trendy and up-to-date. Critics anxious to name a style or define an era ran into formidable opposition in the form of the acid satire of Tom Wolfe in his 1981 book *From Bauhaus to Our House*. Scornful of both trend-setters and their followers, Wolfe dared to make fun of an architecture world that increasingly resembled that of fashion. "Every new $900 000 summer house in the north woods of Michigan or on the shore of Long Island," wrote Wolfe, "has so many pipe railings, ramps, hob-tread metal spiral stairways, sheets of industrial plate glass, banks of tungsten-halogen lamps and white cylindrical shapes, it looks like an insecticide refinery. I once saw the owners of such a place driven to the edge of sensory deprivation by the whiteness & lightness & leanness & cleanness & bareness & spareness of it all. They became desperate for an antidote, such as coziness and color."[1]

It is not that coziness and color are present in every project published here, but *Architecture Now!* has willfully taken the opposite stance from publications (and authors) who seek to make their reputations by defining the style of the moment. It is no accident that John Pawson, the "pope" of minimalism, figures in this book not far from an innovative design for a Floating School in Lagos, Nigeria (NLÉ). At least since the time of the emergence of the International Style of modern architecture, the truth is that there has never really been a dominant trend that could pretend to exclude any others. Thus, *Architecture Now!* is joyously heterogeneous in its guided tour across the world of recent buildings, determined precisely to avoid any scholastic diktat about what should or can be done. It is not that "anything goes," but that the inspirations and reasoning of architects across the world may be more diverse and rich today than they ever have been in the past. The emergence of new economies from China to Brazil has facilitated the development of strong local creativity that has already on occasion attained international recognition. On the other hand, countries such as the United States, once central to contemporary architecture, may have reduced their contribution for a large number of apparently unrelated reasons.

Page 8: Yayoi Kusama, "Love Is Calling," 2013 [p. 226] | Yayoi Kusama, "Infinity Mirrored Room," 2013 [p. 226]

LIGHT YEARS AWAY

Another aspect of the approach of *Architecture Now!* that many readers have noticed in the past is the presence of works of art, not in a fortuitous way, but instead identified at the cusp of the lasting relationship between art and architecture. Artists, even more today than in the fairly recent past, have been fascinated by architectural space, and the contrary is also true of course. In this book, the collaboration between an architect [Arata Isozaki] and the noted artist Anish Kapoor is featured. Developing the idea of sculptures or works that occupy space on an architectural scale, the pair devised Ark Nova, an inflatable concert hall set up in Matsushima close to the areas most damaged by the 2011 Tohoku earthquake and tsunami in Japan [page 264]. Another Japanese artist, Yayoi Kusama, figures here with works shown in New York at David Zwirner in 2013—"Infinity Mirrored Room – the Souls of Millions of Light Years Away," and "Love Is Calling," both 2013 [see page 8 and above]. Light, space, and color are called on by the venerable artist to suggest nearly infinite space, perhaps that of another world, an idea that has fascinated architects for centuries in different forms. So too, the Dutch group RAAAF has sliced through a seemingly impenetrable concrete block to reveal previously unseen space with their work Bunker 599 [Diefdijklinie, the Netherlands, 2010,

page 180]. This piece has a decidedly architectural aspect even if it relies only on cutting an existing structure in two, but so too did the pioneering work of the artist Gordon Matta-Clark. It is not exceedingly common to find works of art in an architecture book, but this is more for reasons of barriers between professions than due to any reality of the creative impulse. Art feeds on architecture and the reverse is, of course, true as well.

TALKING BOOK

When the first volume of *Architecture Now!* was published, the Internet did not permit access to information as easily it does today. Avid users of computers and handheld devices nowadays can get an eyeful of the most contemporary architecture in just seconds. What they may miss, and what hopefully this book provides, is a sense of being guided and not just dropped off in page after page of undifferentiated newness. Those curious enough to look at several of the current architecture blogs on the Internet have surely noticed that the same photos and texts figure in nearly all of them, an emulation not unrelated to the ubiquity of the promotional instinct, as common to artists and movie stars as it is to architects.

There is no doubt that the selling of books has changed radically with the emergence of the

Internet, and also with that of booksellers like Amazon who thrive on instantaneity. Bookshops are becoming rare, especially those animated by a real spirit of discovery or a love for the printed page. But are books any less precious than they were in the past?

DENSITY AND DIVERSITY

It seems apparent that after a relative lull in the construction of innovative large buildings after the 2008 economic slowdown, both pace and size have returned to the scene. One beneficiary of this trend is the Rotterdam office of Rem Koolhaas, OMA. Two of its largest works, De Rotterdam located in the Kop van Zuid area of Rotterdam and the Shenzhen Stock Exchange in China, were completed in 2013. At 162 000 square meters, De Rotterdam is the largest building in the Netherlands, and promotes the idea of a "mixed-use vertical city" [page 114]. Koolhaas is, of course, known for his theories on urban development, promoting density as he did already at the time of the Euralille projects in northern France [1988]. Speaking of De Rotterdam, the architects clearly state: "Urban density and diversity—both in the program and the form—are the guiding principles of the project." The Shenzhen Stock Exchange [page 136] at 265 000 square meters is even larger than De Rotterdam and it experiments in an interesting way with contrasting

elements of regularity and surprise. If the main tower itself seems purely orthogonal and regular, its three-story cantilevered base provokes astonishment if only because of its scale and the 36-meter void that it forms below. Faithful to his own belief that contemporary architecture still has a role to play in the development of cities, Rem Koolhaas states about the Shenzhen Stock Exchange: "We are greatly excited about the building from an architectural standpoint, but I believe its true significance emerges when viewed in an economic, political, and ultimately social context."

Chinese economic growth has, of course, fueled some of the most notable architectural projects of the past years. Another example of this fact is the astonishing Terminal 3 at Shenzhen Bao'an International Airport [see illustration below] by the Rome-based couple Massimiliano and Doriana Fuksas. Although it is true that Fuksas is no stranger to very large projects, having designed and built the one-million-square-meter Trade Fair grounds in Milan [Rho-Pero, Italy, 2002–05], the 500 000-square-meter Shenzhen terminal forces admiration and the daring inspiration of this "organic-shaped sculpture." The double-skin honeycomb design that envelops the building and allows in controlled natural light is a technological feat on this scale, but so, too, is the fact that the architect and his firm realized the interiors of the airport as well. Started in 2010 and completed in 2013, the

Massimiliano and Doriana Fuksas, Terminal 3, Shenzhen Bao'an International Airport, Shenzhen, China, 2010–13 [p. 150]

Ryue Nishizawa, Fukita Pavilion in Shodoshima, Shodoshima, Kagawa, Japan, 2013 [p. 124]

€734 million project stands witness to the formidable construction capacities of the Chinese, but also to the continued presence and inventiveness of architects from the "old continent." Fuksas fancies himself something of an outsider in the closed realm of world-class architects, but it would be surprising if international awards like the Pritzker Prize did not come his way in the near future. Like his friend Renzo Piano, Massimiliano Fuksas has defied the odds to emerge from his native Italy onto the world stage.

ON BILLIONAIRES' ALLEY

Another European architect who has emerged recently on the broader international stage is the 1994 Pritzker Prize winner Christian de Portzamparc. Known principally for his Cité de la Musique (Paris, France, 1985–95) and for a small, elegant tower on 57th Street (LVMH Tower, New York, New York, USA, 1996–99), Portzamparc has unexpectedly returned with a larger concert hall complex in Rio de Janeiro, and a huge tower, like the LVMH building located on 57th Street in Manhattan. It is certain that the rather lyrical qualities of Portzamparc's designs may clash with other thinking in today's architecture, but the Cidade das Artes (Rio de Janeiro, Brazil, 2004–13, page 190), a 46 000-square-meter complex including an 1800-seat Philharmonic Hall and a 1300-seat Opera can be considered a fitting hom-

age to the lyrical use of concrete seen in the work of the late Oscar Niemeyer. The Cidade is located at the crossing of Americas and Ayrton Senna avenues in Rio, an urban hub originally laid out by Lúcio Costa, Niemeyer's mentor and partner in the Brasilia projects. The other, even more surprising Portzamparc realization is One57 (New York, New York, USA, 2010–14, page 82), a huge 306-meter-high residential and hotel tower set just across the street from New York's Carnegie Hall. Indeed, the complex glass façades of the building have a certain musical quality, making the very tall building stand out even more from its relatively low-rise urban environment. With its Park Hyatt Hotel and very luxurious apartments, One57 is among the projects that have made New Yorkers dub 57th Street "Billionaires' Alley," surely in reaction to former New York Mayor Michael Bloomberg's policies in favor of tall residential buildings, a trend that may have slowed significantly with the election of a new mayor.

ARCHITECTURE REIMAGINED

Another frequent feature of the *Architecture Now!* books is temporary, or what might instead be called informal architecture in its various manifestations. This volume is no exception. One of the most talented younger architects in the world, Ryue Nishizawa (born in 1966), has again created a surprising work in Japan. His Fukita

Pavilion in Shodoshima (see opposite page) was created with a surprising simplicity, using just two overlapping, curved sheets of steel. The structure is located on the premises of a shrine and is used as a restaurant and play area for children. Despite its ephemeral appearance and lack of any foundation, the Fukita Pavilion is intended as a permanent structure. Ryue Nishizawa is also the author of one of the most remarkable buildings erected anywhere in the world in recent years, the Teshima Museum (Kagawa, Japan, 2009–10; see *Architecture Now! 8*) which was built on the island that neighbors Shodoshima.

The "Blue Pavilion" (Royal Academy of Arts, London, UK, 2014, page 176) is a more specifically temporary work carried out in the context of an exhibition in London by the excellent young Chilean architects Pezo von Ellrichshausen. The principle of the show "Sensing Spaces: Architecture Reimagined" (January 25 to April 6, 2014) was to demonstrate how much architecture can influence space, and even the moods of visitors. Along with six other architectural firms—including Diébédo Francis Kéré, Eduardo Souto de Moura, Álvaro Siza, Li Xiaodong, and Kengo Kuma, who have all figured prominently in the *Architecture Now!* series—Pezo von Ellrichshausen attracted a great deal of attention with their work. The London daily newspaper *The Independent* wrote: "The first installation by Chilean architects Pezo von Ellrichshausen is a soaring, pine, melodramatic fairy-tale of a structure called Blue. Three large columns rise all the way to the ceiling, impressive and absurd. You

find—unexpectedly—a door at the base of each. You hesitate before entering—is it allowed? You plod up a spiral staircase, which requires effort. You emerge onto a lookout, from whence you can gaze at all the empty space in the room. Most remarkably, you are pressed up close to the gold angels that adorn the neoclassical cornice. This is a metaphysical flourish: you are literally face to face with the divine, usually so out of reach. But then you go down again, and it's a slope this time, and it takes you into a dark corridor with a square of brilliant, shining light at the end, almost like a near-death experience."[2]

SOMEDAY BABY WE'LL BE OLD

Hugh Broughton was born in 1965 in Worcester in the UK. He attended the University of Edinburgh (1984–90) and obtained an M.A. Diploma in Architecture, RIBA, before setting up his own office in London in 1995. Broughton won the 2005 competition to design the first fully relocatable research base intended for the Antarctic. His Halley VI Antarctic Research Station (see illustration below) is an exercise in real flexibility in architectural design. Set on an ice shelf that advances at a rate of 400 meters per year, the 1510-square-meter building must be able to withstand temperatures of -56°C and winds that blow in excess of 160 kilometers per hour. The site can be approached by ship or aircraft during just three months in the summer. Given the rate of movement of the ice shelf, it was necessary that the station could be

Hugh Broughton, Halley VI Antarctic Research Station, Brunt Ice Shelf, Antarctica, 2007–13 (p. 424)

relocated inland as required. Some might say that Halley VI is more an exercise in engineering than it is a work of architecture per se; however, it is through such designs that more mundane forms of construction are able to advance in a technological or ecological sense. Low water and energy usage, as well as careful planning to avoid pollution, are clearly part of this concept. In a worst-case scenario of global climate change, it could well be imagined that buildings such as this one would permit survival in broader areas of extreme weather. Does Halley VI announce a new era where nearly all architecture will be ephemeral?

Sou Fujimoto, Public Toilet in Ichihara, Chiba, Japan, 2012 [p. 132]

A TOILET IN A GARDEN

Imagine that one of the foremost representatives of the rising generation of architects in the world would take enough time to design a public toilet. As is frequently the case with the work of Sou Fujimoto, who was born in 1971, the Public Toilet in Ichihara [see illustration above right] challenges some of the most fundamental assumptions of architecture. Often viewed as leftover spaces that are nonetheless necessary, most public toilets are architecturally indigent. Working near a train station in an area of Japan known for the beauty of its scenery, Fujimoto enclosed an area of 209 square meters with a log fence and actually dared to leave the toilets in a remarkably open, visible place within the perim-

eter. The architect explains: "This multi-layered divergence of internal and external boundaries blends together public and private, the sense of openness and protection, nature and architecture, internal and external, large and small, while retaining their ambiguity." The Japanese do have an unusual interest in toilets, as the very sophisticated products of manufacturers such as Toto attest, and yet the idea of placing such a facility in an open garden is truly astonishing. The Public Toilet in Ichihara is not a temporary installation, but Fujimoto did try his hand in 2013 at an ephemeral design, the Serpentine Gallery Summer Pavilion [see illustration below]. The list of those who have designed these pavilions from

Sou Fujimoto, Serpentine Gallery Summer Pavilion 2013, London, UK, 2013 [p. 306]

NLÉ, Makoko Floating School, Lagos, Nigeria, 2012–13 [p. 430]

year to year reads like a who's who of contemporary architecture. Very open pavilions have been conceived by architects such as SANAA and most recently Herzog & de Meuron of the space near the Serpentine's Georgian gallery in Kensington Gardens. Once again, Fujimoto took an entirely different approach to the assignment, creating a web of 20-millimeter white steel poles erected in a latticework pattern. In its green park setting this structure, which housed a café, was conceived as an invitation to think about the environment. Fujimoto states: "It is a really fundamental question how architecture is different from nature, or how architecture could be part of nature, or how they could be merged . . . what are the boundaries between nature and artificial things."

FROM KADUNA TO ÜRÜMQI

One of the more far-reaching changes that has made itself felt since the first *Architecture Now!* books were published is the geographic spread of the architects concerned and the dispersed realizations of their projects. An interesting example is that of Kunlé Adeyemi who was born in 1976 in Kaduna, Nigeria, where he was raised. He began studying architecture at the University of Lagos at the age of just 16 and was awarded Best Graduating Student of Architecture at the age of 23. He later received a postgraduate degree at Princeton University in New Jersey. Adeyemi continued what has decidedly been a remarkable career

thus far, working in the office of Rem Koolhaas (OMA, Rotterdam) after 2002, where he became a Senior Associate/Design Principal. Rather than remaining in the circuit of prestigious European offices, the young architect chose instead to found his own firm, called NLÉ, in 2010 and engage in a research project on "African Water Cities." The Makoko Floating School (see illustration above) that he designed is a 220-square-meter, open, three-story, A-frame structure that floats on the lagoon of the largest city of Africa. With a population now estimated to surpass 21 million people, Lagos has surpassed Cairo as the biggest population center on the continent. With its play area and classrooms, the Floating School is designed for about 100 elementary-school children, but the simple, inexpensive design could readily be applied to other waterborne uses.

It used to be that the "stars" of contemporary architecture came from predictable places like the USA, the UK, or Italy, for example. Today, the geographic dispersion of architectural talent has reached nearly every corner of the globe. The 2012 Pritzker Prize given to Wang Shu (born in Ürümqi, China, in 1963) is one indication of this trend. In the case of China, government regulations changed, allowing individual architects to have their own practices and not to be systematically integrated into large "institutes" as was the case in the past. Wang Shu's career to date is also an indication that a broadening geographic base of architectural talent by no means implies a homogenization of building design. Wang Shu's most recent project, Tiles Hill (Hangzhou, China, 2011–13, page 458), published here, on the contrary is inspired in part by Chinese tradition, and in particular the tile roofs of a village the architect visited 20 years ago in Hunan Province. The building features rammed-earth walls, strengthened with a steel frame to respect earthquake resistance rules. In a somewhat unexpected comment, Wang Shu explains that this project draws inspiration not only from a celebrated Five Dynasties (907–960) painter but also from the buildings located along the Kamo River in Kyoto: "Layer upon layer, many platforms hang toward the river, as is the case along the Kamo River in Kyoto. In the middle part of the building, there is another path through the whole complex that rises and falls on the way. The third path is on the roof, climbing and winding. Seen from a distance, it reminds me of a work by my favorite Wu Dai Dynasties painter Dong Yuan (ca. 934–962)."

Despite the waning influence of historic modernism in architecture, it is significant that an architect as widely recognized as Wang Shu should derive his influences not from the Bauhaus or Le Corbusier but, on the contrary, from the deep traditions of Asia. Other noted Asian architects, such as Tadao Ando, have clearly made reference to the history of their own countries, but also to the European currents represented in Japan, for example by Bruno Taut and Corbu. Wang Shu's work and the references that he cites are of another order, and this can be taken as an indication of a potentially significant shift in what is considered to be truly "modern" in the chronological sense of the word. Long ago Charles Jencks trumpeted the triumph of postmodernism, but that "school" turned out to be no more than a façade, a pastiche of things apparently too old to be really understood in the contemporary world. Those who know countries like Japan and China realize that ancient traditions are very much present in the same contemporary environment that overflows with neon lights and jangling Pachinko machines.

BIG, Maritime Museum of Denmark, Helsingør, Denmark, 2007–13 (p. 276)

OTHER COUNTRIES, OTHER STORIES

A decade younger than Wang Shu, two high-profile architects are good reasons to look again at countries such as Denmark and Mexico. Bjarke Ingels (born in 1974 in Copenhagen) has proven himself to be a master of a certain form of self-promotion. He lectures frequently and succeeds in convincing those who listen that architecture can once again be exciting and challenging. He compares his Maritime Museum of Denmark (see opposite page) to "a subterranean museum in a dry dock." The 60-year-old dock walls of the site were left untouched, with galleries placed below ground and arranged in a continuous loop around the old walls—making the dock the centerpiece of the exhibition—an open, outdoor area where visitors experience the scale of ship building. Although the very nature of this project and its site did suggest such a possibility, the use of old walls in this context can be considered another harbinger of change. Where real modernism implied a tabula rasa approach and suggested that buildings should appear to sit as lightly on the ground as the Farnsworth House (Ludwig Mies van der Rohe; Plano, Illinois, USA, 1951), Bjarke Ingels not only glorifies old walls, but dares to place museum galleries seven meters below grade.

Tatiana Bilbao is another of the upcoming younger stars of international architecture. She was born in Mexico City in 1972 and graduated in Architecture and Urbanism from the Universidad Iberoamericana in 1996. The Casa Ventura (see illustration above right) is a large (1158 m²) residence that conversely with the previously cited examples finds inspiration in modernism. Bilbao says: "The site reminds us of the image of Modernist houses of the 1950s, photographed by Julius Shulman. This reference was a starting point and an inspiration to begin our design." And yet this is not a place to look for what Tom Wolfe called "the whiteness & lightness & leanness & cleanness & bareness & spareness of it all." A modernist approach might have flattened this site and made it uniform. "Instead," says Tatiana Bilbao, "of creating a house that is over the hill-side, we have built a house that is part of it, grows from it, and becomes part of the composition of the natural environment." Even more contrary

Tatiana Bilbao, Casa Ventura, Monterrey, Mexico, 2010–11 [p. 32]

to the Euclidean approach of modernism, the architects also state that the design is inspired by funguses that grow on trees and "somehow become part of them."

TURBULENCE IN THE GRID

The strengthening influence of natural forms on contemporary architecture, surely rendered more significant because of computer-assisted design and manufacturing, was underlined by the 2013–14 exhibition "Naturalizing Architecture," curated by Marie-Ange Brayer, Director of the FRAC Centre Orléans, together with Frédéric Migayrou, head of the Architecture department at the Pompidou Center, who is also Chair and Professor of Architecture at the Bartlett School of Architecture, London. This show mixed the work of relatively well-known practices, such as that of Junya Ishigami or the Beijing group MAD, with much younger and less experienced teams from all over the world. Describing the characteristics of the works chosen, the curators stated: "Today, through recourse to the most advanced digital

Jakob + MacFarlane, Les Turbulences, FRAC Centre, Orléans, France, 2010–13 [p. 246]

tecture for a number of years, it can be said that today the techniques and the design comprehension required to work in this way are reaching a certain maturity. From the early "blobs" that had little to recommend them aside from their lack of Euclidean coordinates, computer design has evolved to the point where genuinely new forms have emerged, often bringing with them, as is the case for the FRAC Centre, a real relationship to the site and to the functioning of the institution concerned.

tools, architects envisage projects which evolve according to principles similar to those found in nature. In close proximity to science, they develop a high level of proficiency in mathematics, which enables them to artificially simulate formation and growth processes unique to the kingdom of life. . . . Architects now develop a practice at the crossroads of design, computer science, engineering, and biology. Conditions for production in the domain of architecture are radically redefined by this convergence, as well as by the constant evolution of the processes and tools for digital manufacturing. For the first time, these new design processes which integrate the fields of robotics, nanotechnology, genetics, and biotechnology are presented through the research of a new generation."[3]

"Naturalizing Architecture" was the inaugural exhibition in the new FRAC Centre building (see illustration above) by the Paris-based team Jakob + MacFarlane. As they have in the past, the architects employed a computer-assisted design technique that consists in a manipulation of grids that exist on the site. "We identified two predominate grids emanating from the historic context of the site. The meeting and the convergence of these two geometries materializes in a deformation, a zone of turbulence, the future presence of the FRAC Centre." Though computer-driven design has been a factor in contemporary archi-

NOT AN INSECTICIDE REFINERY

An interesting, nearly total contrast with the work of Jakob + MacFarlane can be found in the most recent work of John Pawson, celebrated not only because of his numerous projects for high-profile clients, but also for his seminal 1996 book

John Pawson, St. Moritz Church Interior Remodeling, Augsburg, Germany, 2011–13 [p. 318]

Eduardo Souto de Moura, Multipurpose Pavilion, Viana do Castelo, Portugal, 2009–13 [p. 370]

Minimum. In the same spirit as he had earlier with the renovation of a wing of the Abbey of Our Lady of Nový Dvůr [Czech Republic, 2004; Phase 2, 2009], or the church renovation concerning the lateral sacristy and chapels of the Abbey of Our Lady of Sept-Fons [Burgundy, France, 2009], Pawson took on the challenge of remodeling the interior of the St. Moritz Church [Augsburg, Germany, 2011–13, page 318]. Founded in 1019, St. Moritz is the oldest church in Augsburg. Seeking to "pare away" selected artifacts in order to "clear the visual field," Pawson reinforced the architectural focus on the apse of the church. Glass in the apse windows was replaced with thin pieces of onyx, creating a luminous environment for a Baroque sculpture, the *Christus Salvator* by Georg Petel. The architects explain: "The treatment of the apse windows represents the culmination of a wider strategy for light, whose aim is to achieve a clear distribution of light, with the apse as the brightest area in the church. After the apse, the area of the nave where the liturgy is performed is brightest, while the aisles revert to more subdued light conditions. The Baroque clerestory windows, relieved of their former function of illuminating the artwork and decoration, now serve as indirect sources of light." Far from Wolfe's "insecticide refinery," Pawson's minimalism floods this church with real light, while his eye for simplicity brings the focus back to some of the founding ideas of the church. This project may not make minimalism as popular as it once was in architecture and interior design, but it does clearly make the point that history can be brought together with representations of the modern that are respectful of space and time.

In *Architecture Now! Vol. 10*, Jakob + MacFarlane can coexist peacefully with John Pawson. Though style is surely not often a matter of age, Dominique Jakob is 17 years younger than John Pawson and her vision of architecture has been formed by the likes of Thom Mayne [Morphosis]. There are certainly trends and sources of inspiration that run like rivers through contemporary architecture, but there are many rivers. Selecting one and declaring it to be the "flavor of the moment" is a facile gesture, perhaps as superficial as was postmodernism. The reality of architecture is much more complex and evolves constantly, continuing, for example, to break through previously isolated disciplines, as the "Naturalizing Architecture" show demonstrated.

IS THERE LIFE AFTER THE PRITZKER?

For some architects, winning the Pritzker Prize is the culmination of their professional life, and those who do not win are left in a permanent state of expectation or jealousy. Others, like the two Portuguese laureates Álvaro Siza (1992) and Eduardo Souto de Moura (2011), feel that they are excluded from projects in their own country precisely because they have won the prestigious prize. Is there life after the Pritzker? In the case of two winners with recent works in this volume of *Architecture Now!*, there clearly is a life after. The first of these is Souto de Moura himself with his Multipurpose Pavilion (see previous page). This 5942-square-meter structure is located in the heart of what might be considered a high point of contemporary Portuguese architecture, because it is near buildings by Fernando Távora (Praça da Liberdade) and Álvaro Siza (Public Library, 2001–07). Nearly 40 years after the tubes and pipes of the Pompidou Center (Renzo Piano + Richard Rogers; Paris, France, 1977) raised an uproar among those who find contemporary architecture useless, Souto de Moura has in some sense returned to the scene of the crime and allowed ducts to run along the full length of his otherwise very elegant building. But these are not the multicolored tubes of Beaubourg, they are straight and clean and silvery. Slightly more square than its Parisian counterpart, this "aluminum box" also makes reference to naval architecture, and admits sports among the uses for its open volumes. Well, yes, this building is 15 times smaller than Beaubourg, but it shows an elegance and calmness that escaped the young future Pritzker Prize winners Piano (1998) and Rogers (2007).

WHY NOT WHITE?

Another slightly older Pritzker winner, Richard Meier (1984), continues to design remarkable buildings that are very much in the lines of those that made his reputation many years ago. His United States Courthouse (see illustration to the right) is a large (43 082 m²) building that includes a 16-story tower and an elliptical glass-roofed lobby. Rather than the pure white that he has often employed, Richard Meier used natural stone and terracotta, together with concrete, to give the building a "Mediterranean quality of place." Unlike the grand white ships of earlier times, this one has received a LEED Gold certification for its strict adherence to the principles of sustain-

ability. Actually, when Tom Wolfe was writing about "every new $900 000 summer house in the north woods of Michigan . . ." he was thinking very precisely about Richard Meier's often-published Douglas House (Harbor Springs, Michigan, USA, 1971–73). It was Leon Trotsky in his response to the Mensheviks at the Petrograd Second Congress of the Soviets (October 25, 1917) who ranted: "You are pitiful, isolated individuals! You are bankrupts. Your role is played out. Go where you belong from now on—into the dustbin of history!" And what if whiteness and geometric plans did not have to be relegated to the "dustbin of history"? What if the spareness and light of John Pawson, or the white of Meier were related to more than the fashion of a (past) moment? Richard Meier wrote: "White is the ephemeral emblem of perpetual movement. The white is always present but never the same, bright and rolling in the day, silver and effervescent under the full moon of New Year's Eve. Between the sea of consciousness and earth's vast mate-riality lies this ever-changing line of white. White is the light, the medium of understanding and transformative power."

Richard Meier, United States Courthouse, San Diego, California, USA, 2003–13 (p. 164)

IT'S THE BUILDING, STUPID

It will not be argued that style never matters or that time does not go by, but rather that architecture in particular should not be and is not subjected to the rules that apply to this year's length of skirt. Finally and fundamentally, this argument also impinges on the myth of the "star architect." Pritkzer Prize winners from Meier to Jean Nouvel (2008) have cultivated, much as Frank Lloyd Wright did in his time, the notion of personality and specific style as keys to their success. In the final analysis it all comes down to the buildings, and how they pass through time. One might paraphrase Bill Clinton and remind fans and followers of men in black hats that the real gage of architectural success is what stands and remains—it's the building, stupid.

Well, surprise, Jean Nouvel actually makes terrific buildings, as his long-awaited Doha Tower (see illustration to the right) demonstrates. This 231-meter-high cylindrical tower stands near the center of the Qatari city's West Bay downtown area and bears more than a passing resemblance to Nouvel's Torre Agbar, built on the equally symbolic Avenida Diagonal in Barcelona in 2000. The client for the Doha Tower was Sheikh Saud bin Mohammed bin Ali Al Thani, known in art-world circles for his active promotion of cultural projects in the Emirate, culminating in the construction of I. M. Pei's Museum of Islamic Art (2008). The Sheikh had his own entrance to the building on the inland side, and occupied levels 43 and 44 of the structure under the dome. The building has an unusual entrance configuration—with a sloping, landscaped ramp leading down to the main entrances that are below grade and covered by a circular canopy. As seen from street level, the building in fact appears to have no entrance—it becomes a purely sculptural object on the West Bay skyline, showing no visible surfaces in glass, and with a sunken garden emerging at street level. Complemented by a sophisticated LED lighting system imagined by Yann Kersalé, the Doha Tower stands out against what might best be described as a zoo of skyscraper forms on the West Bay skyline, a calm yet forceful presence, clad in a metal web of varying density that blocks the burning sun. Nouvel is in the process of building an even more surprising structure at

Jean Nouvel, Doha Tower, Doha, Qatar, 2007–11 [p. 118]

the opposite end of Doha's Corniche, the National Museum of Qatar, which should reach completion at about the same time as the Louvre Abu Dhabi in another nearby Gulf Emirate.

GOING WITH THE FLOW IN BAKU

An obvious shift in economics has thus had its impact on contemporary architecture, drawing "big name" designers to places that most Europeans or Americans have hardly ever heard of. Significant buildings do often spring up where capital flows most readily, but it remains a challenge to create excellent architecture where local culture is not necessarily in harmony with Western creativity. Another Pritzker Prize winner, and to date the only woman to win the award on her own, Zaha Hadid (2004), has just completed the Heydar Aliyev Center (see following page). Zaha Hadid Architects were appointed design architects of the Heydar Aliyev Center as a result of a 2007 competition. It is intended as the main building for the country's cultural programs. Making use of a solid external skin made of fiberglass-reinforced polyester rain-screen cladding panels,

Zaha Hadid, Heydar Aliyev Center, Baku, Azerbaijan, 2012 (p. 216) | Page 25: Massimiliano and Doriana Fuksas, New National Archives of France, 2009–13 (p. 292)

Hadid creates unified, flowing façades, while carefully respecting the unusual site configuration. Zaha Hadid Architects go to considerable lengths to explain (justify?) the unexpected form of the Heydar Aliyev Center. They write: "Fluidity in architecture is not new to this region. In historical Islamic architecture, rows, grids, or sequences of columns flow to infinity like trees in a forest, establishing non-hierarchical space. Continuous calligraphic and ornamental patterns flow from carpets to walls, walls to ceilings, ceilings to domes, establishing seamless relationships and blurring distinctions between architectural elements and the ground they inhabit. Our intention was to relate to that historical understanding of architecture, not through the use of mimicry or a limiting adherence to the iconography of the past, but rather by developing a firmly contemporary interpretation, reflecting a more nuanced understanding." In fact, the fluidity of the architecture, and even more precisely its forms, is coherent with the thinking and other realizations of Zaha Hadid, no matter what their geographic or historical context.

THE GRID AND THE PATHWAY

Does rootedness have any place in the discourse of contemporary architecture? It is obvious that when Wang Shu speaks of the tile roofs of a village he visited in Hunan, the cultural reference has a justifiable bearing on what he is doing in the Tiles Hill project. Although the Iraqi-born Hadid obviously knows the culture of Islam, it may be asked if the flowing continuity of which she speaks is more closely related to Baku or to her own, personal style. Then again, the problem may not be so much architecture as it is the societies on which it is founded. Prada stores traditionally change their windows all over the world to the same presentation simultaneously. What if the "world logic" that applies to Coca-Cola or Apple computers had finally, definitively gained the world of architecture. After all, one tower in Doha looks very much like another in Barcelona. Again, there are as many responses to the question of "local color" in architecture as there are architects. Some discourse is as superficial as postmodernism in its reference to history and place, while other, more subtle architects still actively seek the genius loci.

In yet another effort to render the analysis of contemporary architecture systematic, the Columbia University Professor Kenneth Frampton has recently returned in the magazine *Domus* to comment on his influential 1983 essay "Six Points for an Architecture of Resistance." Itself influenced by the work of Alex Tzonis and Liane Lefaivre ("The Grid and the Pathway," 1981), Frampton's piece laid out the case for what has been called "Critical Regionalism," an approach that seeks to mediate between the global and the local expressions of architecture, at once rejecting the lack of identity that was part and parcel of the fallout from modernism and the flourishes of ornamentation so close to the heart of Jencks. Thirty years on, Frampton writes: "The bulk of contemporary practice is global rather than local, with star architects traveling incessantly all over the world in pursuit of the equally dynamic flow of capital. Herein we witness the vox populi's susceptibility to the mediagenic impact of spectacular form which is as much due to the capacity of 'superstar architects' to come up with sensational, novel images as to their organizational competence and technical ability. Hence, the advent of the so-called Bilbao effect, where cities and institutions compete with each other in order to sponsor a building designed by a recognizable brand name." Specifically critical of "a world in which cities rival each other for the dubious honor of sponsoring the highest building in the world, the title being held, as of now, by Dubai which, while barely a city at all, has nonetheless to its renown the 160-story Burj Tower," the author goes on to cite regional offices like Studio Mumbai as an effective antidote. "Thus, for me," Kenneth Frampton concludes, "a liberative promise for the future resides in an agonistic architecture of the periphery as opposed to the subtle nonjudgmental conformism of ruling taste emanating from the center. . . . By the term 'agonistic' I wish to evoke the idea of an architecture which continues to place emphasis on the particular brief and on the specific nature of the topography and climate in which it is situated, while still giving high priority to the expressivity and the physical attributes of the material out of which the work is made."[4]

NOTHING SUCCEEDS LIKE EXCESS

Frampton, born in 1930, carries with him a good deal of pessimism about contemporary society in general and his analysis appears to focus on very specific examples that naturally tend to confirm his theses. There is undoubtedly an "apparatus" of contemporary architecture that is closely related to capital flows and to the prevailing economic system, especially when buildings of a certain size are concerned. The system "fabricates" or allows the rise of "superstar architects" sometimes only to fire on them for such excellent reasons as "cost overruns." Both Jean Nouvel (Philharmonie de Paris) and Herzog & de Meuron (Elbphilharmonie Hamburg) were caught up in precisely this kind of economic debate as this book went to press, despite their undeniable talents. Rather than trying to bring forth an "agnostic architecture" by the force of criticism, might it not be useful to note that the very system that Frampton criticizes also seems to accept the presence of architects like Wang Shu or Studio Mumbai, both originating in rising economies with long traditions and rich histories.

Criticism takes on an established order, or the work of a given architect and proceeds to attempt to demolish its interest if not its substance. At the same time, it is a formidable task to even begin to become aware of what is happening around the earth. Architecture of considerable interest has begun to pop up all over the world as it were, and despite globalized information and relatively easy travel, few can even begin to have an overview of the different expressions of reality, let alone seek to relegate an architect or a class of architects to the dustbin of history. Kenneth Frampton may reveal the real source of his malaise when he cites Jean Baudrillard, who, at a 1986 symposium entitled "Looking Back on the End of the World," at Columbia University, stated: "We are no longer in a state of growth; we are in a state of excess. We are living in a society of excrescence, meaning that which incessantly develops without being measurable against its own objectives. The boil is growing out of control, recklessly at cross-purposes with itself, its impacts multiplying as the causes disintegrate. . . . This satiation has nothing to do with the excess of which Bataille spoke, which all societies have managed to produce and destroy in useless and wasteful exhaustion. . . . We no longer know how we can possibly use up all these accumulated things; we no longer even know what they are for. Every factor of acceleration and concentration brings us closer to the point of inertia."[5]

MONEY MAKES THE WORLD GO ROUND

Is it not this identification of much (most?) contemporary architecture with a society of excess and waste that makes Frampton and others so critical of what is happening today? Once again, *Architecture Now! Vol. 10* includes both the Shenzhen Stock Exchange and a Floating School that serves Lagos. How interesting and unexpected that the Stock Exchange is the work of OMA, the same office where the architect of the Floating School gained much of his knowledge. Nor, of course should it be suggested that this volume or any other can actually come to terms with the contemporary architecture of the world. Any seasoned traveler with an interest in architecture knows how few and far between good buildings are in any city. Most new buildings are intellectually derivative, cookie cutter forms from the age of mass standardization, which today has come to an end. The real negative influence on architecture is also its raison d'être, which is to say finally, money. Clients, promoters and builders squeeze every last penny from their projects, often resulting in what might best be called a bastardization of the architect's original idea. It often seems clear that a "good" architect is the one who can succeed in having his scheme brought to fruition as he conceived it. Knowing how to reach that conclusion is the test that separates an intellectual approach to the profession from a practical and valid one. Just as some visitors may stare up at the 828-meter-high Burj Khalifa in Dubai and be astonished at a feat of human achievement, others may be depressed by the waste it apparently represents. The only real antidote to mediocrity or excess is a thoughtful process of observation, shared and disseminated widely enough to have an impact. Grumbling at the world as it is will not solve many problems; looking at what has been built with an open mind might just help to improve the future.

1   Tom Wolfe, *From Bauhaus to Our House*, Farrar Straus Giroux, New York, 1981.
2   Zoe Pilger, "'Sensing Spaces: Architecture Reimagined,' review: 'A terrific show that leaves you at peace,'"
The Independent, February 15, 2014, http://www.independent.co.uk/arts-entertainment/art/reviews/sensing-spaces-architecture-reimagined-review-a-terrific-show-that-leaves-you-at-peace-9090890.html, accessed on January 12, 2015.
3   http://www.frac-centre.fr/_en/archilab-492.html, accessed on January 12, 2015.
4   Kenneth Frampton, "Towards an Agonistic Architecture," originally published in *Domus* 972, September 2013,
http://www.domusweb.it/en/op-ed/2013/10/03/_towards_an_agonistic_architecture.html, accessed on January 12, 2015.
5   Jean Baudrillard, cited in Kenneth Frampton, "Towards an Agonistic Architecture," originally published in *Domus* 972,
September 2013.

RES
IDEN
TIAL

CASA VENTURA by TATIANA BILBAO

Andreas Fuhrimann Gabrielle Hächler

ARTIST'S HOUSE

2010–12

LOCATION Würenlos, Switzerland — **AREA** 400 m²
CLIENT Ugo Rondinone — **COLLABORATION** Ugo Rondinone, Gilbert Isermann

This house for the well-known artist Ugo Rondinone is surrounded on three sides by woodland, and stands on the periphery of the small village of Würenlos near Zurich. The north façade has a porch and is parallel to a stream, and the two-story living room faces a garden space with an oak in its center. On the sloped terrain, the architects inserted technical rooms, a sauna, and cellar space below grade. Terraces surround the structure, which, according to the architects, confers a lightness that is reminiscent of traditional Japanese wooden houses. Cantilevered canopies are also part of the design. The main ground level is occupied by the living room, kitchen, library, and a bedroom and bathroom with direct garden access. The living room has a functioning "Georgianstyle" New York fireplace that is a work by the artist. The Artist's House was built with prefabricated wood elements and is clad with untreated materials, such as corrugated Eternit for the roof and white plaster inside.

The interiors of the building borrow from a number of different architectural typologies, including the industrial shed. Natural light is given priority in working space (above), while a living area with generous volume contrasts a large opening and white walls with a wooden floor.

The forms of the house are at once relatively
simple and yet features such as the angled skylight,
seen above, bring a good deal of sophistication
and surprise to the interiors.

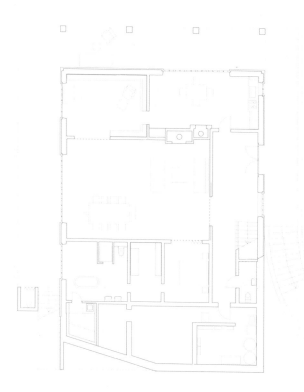
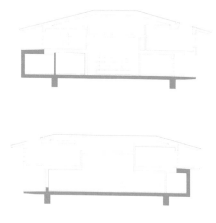

A floor plan and elevation views
of the house show its slight devia-
tions from the purely orthogonal
box, with a roof that has two sloping elements and an orchestration
of interior spaces that juxtaposes
closed, private areas with the
larger more public living area near
the center of the house.

Tatiana Bilbao

CASA VENTURA

2010-11

LOCATION Monterrey, Mexico — **AREA** 1158 m²
COST $2 million — **COLLABORATION** Paralelo (Construction Company)

The architects say that the building's location in a suburb of the city with a view of Monterrey reminded them "of the image of Modernist houses of the 1950s, photographed by Julius Shulman," and that "this reference was a starting point and an inspiration." Charged with creating a

single-story structure with a clear division between public and private spaces, as well as an orientation that would promote energy savings, each zone of the largely concrete residence is defined within a pentagon that is deformed to allow for views and movement within the house, as well as the complex topography. Public areas are located on the flattest portion of the site, and a spiral staircase connects it to the private spaces. "Instead of creating a house that is over the hillside, we have built a house that is part of it, grows from it, and becomes part of the composition of the natural environment," state the architects. "Casa Ventura is more than a house; it is a lab of architectonic experiences whose only intention is to create a pleasant family life, and that responds to the joyful and dynamic life the family lives and their needs."

The symbiotic relationship of the house with its site is developed through the angled interior spaces, inner courtyards, and broad glazing.

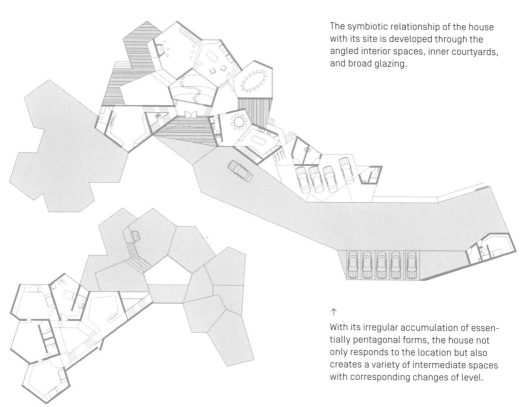

↑

With its irregular accumulation of essentially pentagonal forms, the house not only responds to the location but also creates a variety of intermediate spaces with corresponding changes of level.

COURTYARD HOUSE

2012–13

LOCATION Aurora, Oregon, USA — **AREA** 231 m^2 — **COST** $585 000
COLLABORATION Curtis Bosworth (GC), Jerome Madden (Structural), Alexander Prixdeaux (Landscape)

Located on a hillside overlooking protected wetlands, this residence cantilevers the Pudding River at one end, and digs into the landscape at the other. It is entered through an underground garage court, and has living spaces that flow in a continuous loop around two L-shaped storage cores and a faceted glass courtyard, which brings light and air into the subterranean interiors of the house. The architect describes it in these words: "Rather than a series of

The house is nestled into its sloping site, with a large angled opening in the middle of the flat roof creating space for an interior courtyard (following double page) that brings even more natural light into the structure.

wasted bedrooms separated from living, during the day the Courtyard House can be experienced as a single loft with every room becoming a living space, while at night every space can become a private sleeping room." The Courtyard House was the first freestanding building completed by NO Architecture and is meant to "sponsor more collective and ecological forms of life without sacrificing the necessary privacy of daily living."

Although when seen from some angles the house has decided contrasts between opacity and transparency (above), interior views show that it is largely opened to its natural setting (below).

A north section drawing of the house is seen with a similar photo of the completed structure (below). The horizontality of the design creates relatively little disturbance in the natural topography, but nonetheless declares its modernity.

Bercy Chen

EDGELAND HOUSE

2011–12

LOCATION Austin, Texas, USA
AREA 130 m² — **COLLABORATION** Huan Zheng

Edgeland House is "a modern reinterpretation of one of the oldest housing typologies in North America, the Native American Pit House," that the architects refer to as "site-specific installation art." Set on a rehabilitated brownfield site, the sunken structure takes advantage of the earth to

regulate thermal comfort, being inserted about two meters into the earth, and also contains an insulating green room, while an integrated hydronic HVAC system further increases energy efficiency. There are two separate pavilions, for living and sleeping, requiring direct contact with the outside elements to pass from one area to the other. Bercy Chen worked with the Lady Bird Johnson Wildflower Center to reintroduce more than 40 native species of plants and wildflowers to the house's green roof and site.

↑
The overall form of the house is articulated around a central open space and large angular glass volumes.

↓
In the plan, the nearly triangular swimming pool visible on the previous double page forms an integral part of the composition.

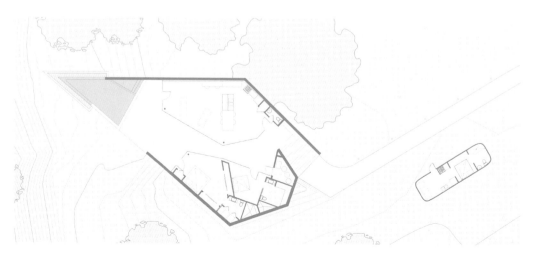

ELK RUN RIDGE

2012

LOCATION Churchville, Augusta County, Virginia, USA
AREA 402 m² — **COLLABORATION** Gregg Bleam (Landscape Architect)

A folk art dealer and a music teacher called on the architects to build what they called an "instant heirloom" to display their collection and to organize large annual reunions. Set on a hill in the midst of 40 hectares of farmland and intended to be "functional for two people or 150 people," Elk Run Ridge has cedar and fieldstone walls, concrete floors with radiant heating linked to a geothermal system, and a zinc roof, as well as a good deal of glazing. Built-in shelving and furniture are part of an overall scheme that combines careful attention to energy savings while also giving importance to handmade crafts and local culture.

A combination essentially made up of wood, stone,
and glass in the double-height living space provides open
views of the site with broad high glazing.

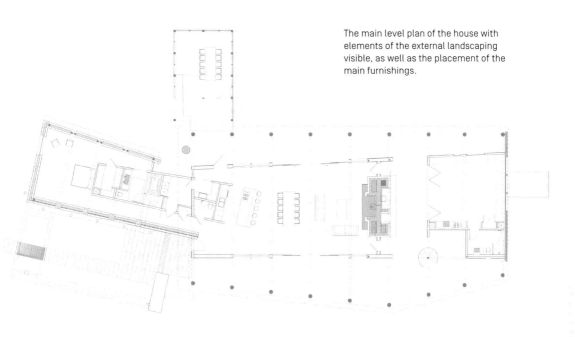

The main level plan of the house with elements of the external landscaping visible, as well as the placement of the main furnishings.

↓
A bedroom confirms the material contrasts seen in the public spaces with the warm walnut clad "basket weave" core of the structure and fieldstone wall visible to the right of the image.

Thiago Bernardes

GCP HOUSE

2012–13

LOCATION Porto Feliz, São Paulo, Brazil
AREA 910 m²

According to the architects, the essential features of the architecture of this large weekend house located 70 kilometers from the city of São Paulo in the province of Porto Feliz are a "contrast between volumes, interior-exterior transition spaces, a diversity of construction materials and techniques, the use of color, and generous views." Copper sheets are used to clad walls of the "social pavilion" and bedroom area. The volume housing the bedrooms is a reinforced-concrete box with generous openings to let light and air into the sleeping areas and bathroom. It is raised 40 centimeters above the ground to avoid rising ground dampness and to convey a feeling of "intimacy and privacy." The social or public area is a light timber structure with wood columns supporting glulam timber beams and a tilting, light roof with long spans and cantilevers. This wooden structure shares its stone flooring with the outside terrace, doing away with the obvious limits between interior and exterior and making this part of the GCP House more extroverted.

The architects list copper and wood as being the main materials used in this house, a statement fully underlined by the images on the left page with the pivoting doors seen in the open position.

↓
A ground floor plan of the house with the bedroom aligned to the lower left and the dining room, living area, veranda, and pool in the upper part of the drawing.

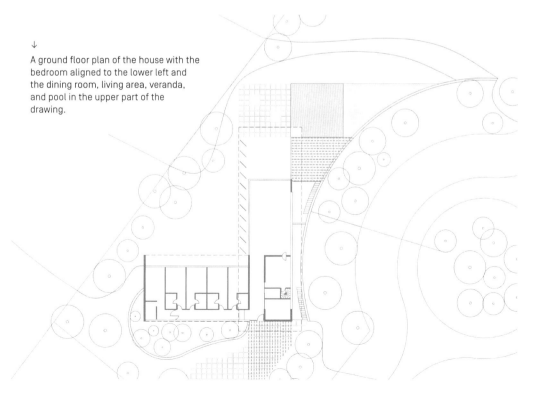

Javier Corvalán

HAMACA HOUSE

2009

LOCATION Ingavi c/Marilien, Luque, Paraguay
AREA 80 m² — **CLIENT** Francisco Oddone — **COST** $25 000

Hamaca House is named after the form of the hammock that inspired it. Built on a 360-square-meter site, two brick-clad blocks at either end "counterbalance" the galvanized-steel roof. These massive tilted blocks forming opposite ends of the structure are mirrored inside where the central space is essentially open, with the steel roof connecting and protecting this intermediate space. A closed area is contrasted with this large open, or "intermediate," space with a kitchen and barbecue. Despite its unusual statics, the house has a simple, rectangular, "hammock-shape" floor plan.

A floor plan of the house shows the central kitchen area and the barbecue space to the right. A patio continues outdoors to the right of the barbecue.

HOUSE 36

2012–14

LOCATION Stuttgart, Germany
AREA 377 m²

Made entirely of insulated concrete, House 36 is the first of its type in Germany. Both exterior walls and the faceted roof are made of this poured-in-place material that obviates the need for supplementary insulation. The insulated concrete is made by replacing pebble stone aggregates with recycled foam glass granulate and 20% air bubbles in the mix. Walls are 45 to 50 centimeters thick, and permit the house to be warm in winter and cool in summer. The architect's design unites insulation and the technical installations in the single-layer walls that were cast with rough-sawn formwork to create "a rich and sound surface aesthetically similar to a natural stone wall and delicately contrasting with the massive natural wood panels framing the openings on the inside." Surrounded by older stone houses, the "mountain crystal" shape of this new residence sits on a steep, north-facing slope.

←
The architects call this a "monolithic building that almost resembles a mountain crystal." Insulating concrete is used throughout, obviating the need for further "thermal barriers."

Right, the west elevation of the house, and below, two section drawings.

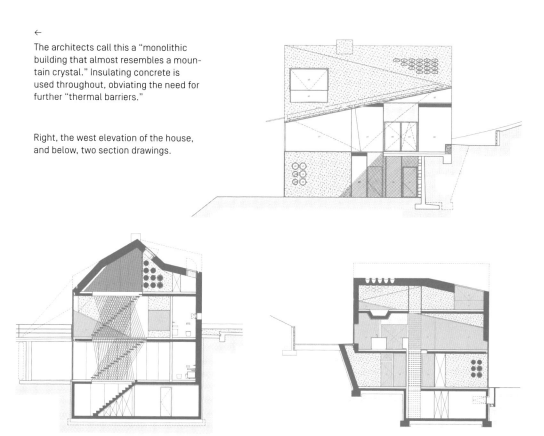

#HOUSE#1.130

2011–13

LOCATION Madrid, Spain — **AREA** 500 m²
COLLABORATION Alvar Ruiz Villanueva (Associate Architect)

This single-family residence set on a long, narrow, south-sloping site was carried out as a design-build project by entresitio. As the architects explain, the design consists of "two different schemes superimposed one on top of the other: a longitudinal one, based on spatial forking, and another underneath, based on a hand and fingers-like configuration." The upper level is a public or day pavilion with a metal roof and concrete and glass walls, while the private rooms are set below, like "nested openings." Fragmentation of the volumes allows natural light to penetrate throughout, while a "permeable skin" heightens an impression of blurred boundaries between interior and exterior. The architects call it a "formless project" because it is impossible to have a full volumetric comprehension of the design from any single point of view.

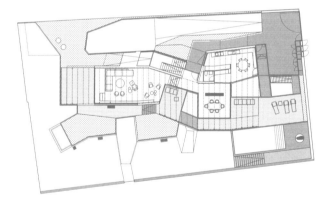

←
The upper and lower level plans of the house show its complexity and give a hint of its size. The architects state that "supporting elements are secondary and intentionally hidden and as thin as possible," as seen in the image above.

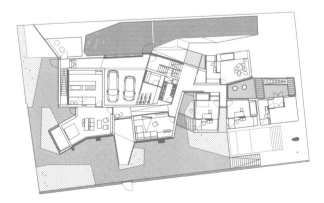

→

Light filters into nearly every part of the interior, here bathing a simple wooden table and chairs in sunlight.

↓

The metal roof structure, seen in the image below, gives visual continuity to the upper level. Concrete supporting walls and the glass enclosure are the only two vertical elements seen in the design.

Wiel Arets

JELLYFISH HOUSE

2013

LOCATION Marbella, Spain — AREA 650 m²
COLLABORATION Bettina Kraus, Lars Dreessen, Dennis Villanueva

Since neighboring buildings block the view of Jellyfish House to the sea, it was decided to cantilever the house's pool from its roof nine meters, so that the beach and sea can be seen while sunbathing or swimming. The pool has a glass bottom, panoramic window on its interior side, and an "infinity edge" that makes it appear to merge with the sea in the distance. As the architects explain, "the house is organized around two paths of circulation: a 'fast' and 'slow' set of stairs, which intertwine and traverse the house's four levels of living." There are five bedrooms, with two guest rooms on the lowest level. The kitchen is placed along the southern façade of the house on the first floor, which also houses the sauna and steam bath. Poured-in-place white concrete was used, along with substantial glazing. Most of the façades of the house can be opened, and its staircases are in good part outside.

The rooftop swimming pool makes its presence felt within
the house, where a large underwater window reveals swimmers
to those inside the residence.

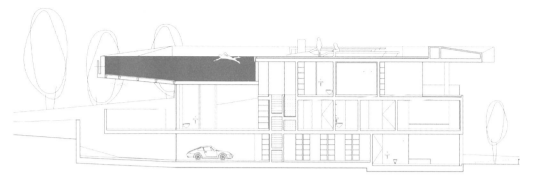

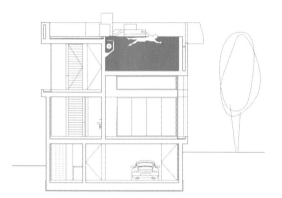

↑

Section drawings show the three levels of the house and the swimming pool.

↓

The stairway penetrates the structure creating contrasts between a stony solidity and large glazed openings.

Tham & Videgård

LAGNÖ SUMMER HOUSE

2012

LOCATION Lagnö, Sweden
AREA 140 m²

The Lagnö Summer House is set between a forest and the coastline of the Stockholm archipelago. A sequence of interconnected, pitched roofs made of cast concrete create interior spaces of varying size and height—small rooms for the entrance, kitchen, sleeping area, and bathroom form a thick wall toward the north, while a continuous open space for living and dining is situated to the south, with open views of the neighboring islands, the Baltic Sea, and the horizon. An unexpected effect is achieved on this southern exposure with the apparently heavy concrete roofs suspended over a very light ground floor made of glass and wood with broad, opening, glazed doors.

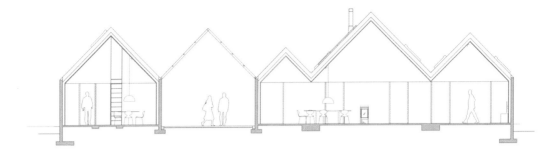

↑
A section view of the north façade of the house shows its successive double-slope roofs.

↓
A plan with the terrace and pool at the bottom and a guest space and atelier on the left.

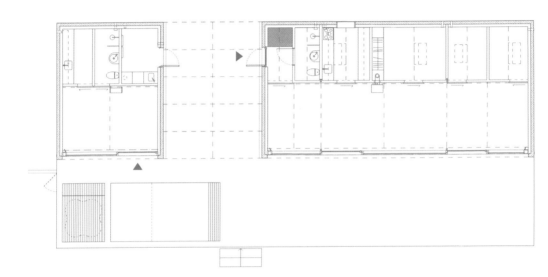

The multiple roof arrangement creates interesting angled interior spaces. In the public areas (above and bottom left), full-height glazing brings ample natural light into the residence.

ONE57

2010–14

LOCATION 157 West 57th Street, New York, NY 10019, USA, www.one57.com
AREA 74 350 m² — **CLIENT** Extell Development Company

This 75-story, 306-meter-high tower dominates its neighborhood on West 57th Street in Manhattan, on an unusual L-shaped site just across the street from Carnegie Hall. The project was based on a 2005 direct commission from Gary Barnett, President of the Extell Development Company. Heights up to 400 meters were envisaged during the development process, and the completed tower remains one of the tallest residential buildings in Manhattan. Aside from luxurious apartments on the upper floors, One57 includes the Park Hyatt Hotel. Residential interior design was by Thomas Juul-Hansen, while the hotel interior is by Yabu Pushelberg. As he did for the earlier LVMH Tower also located on 57th Street, the architect carefully studied the city's alignment regulations and the air rights specific to this site, describing the project in the following words: "The building's volumes are linked by an ascending and descending cascading movement that flows over curved transitional surfaces containing inhabited terraces. A vertical pattern of contrasting stripes comprised of two different glass types (with uniform visibility from the interior) distinguish the north façades and recall the vertical energy of New York's cascading skyline, in contrast with the east and west façades that resemble the aesthetic of the Le Monde and Nantes projects."

← One57 dominates its immediate street setting, as seen on the left page, but other tall towers are planned for the area. Left, the structure seen from Columbus Circle.

↓ Models show the configuration that was carefully studied to correspond to New York City's zoning laws.

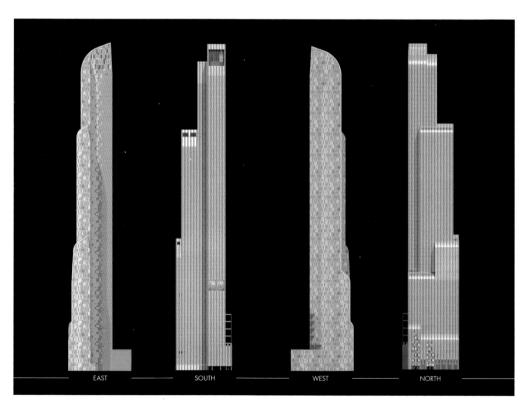

EAST   SOUTH   WEST   NORTH

SOLO HOUSE

2013

LOCATION Cretas, Spain
AREA 313 m² — **CLIENT** Christian Bourdais, Solo Houses

Built in a rural landscape of vineyards and olive groves, this horizontal design is "detached from the ground, suspended in an almost archaic time," according to the designers. Entered via a straight, sloping path, the house is marked by bifurcated steps—"like going into a twin tunnel that encircles the central swimming pool, with small openings set diagonally that allow glimpses of sky across the water." Sixteen columns placed at regular intervals define the perimeter of the house, while a sequence of symmetrical rooms with undefined functions are arrayed behind these columns with four open terraces at the corners. The only closed room in the design is at the center: it has no roof and water serves as its "floor." The project is part of the Solo Houses, a group of 12 residences being designed by architects such as Sou Fujimoto, Studio Mumbai, and TNA. The Pezo von Ellrichshausen Solo House is the first of these to be completed.

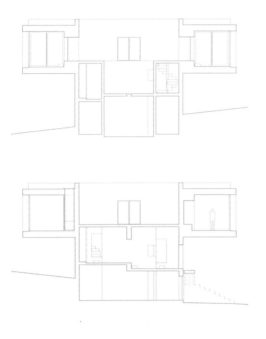

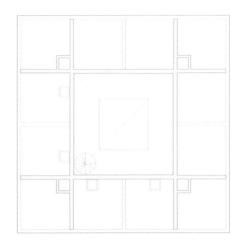

To the right, the top, third, and second
floor plans of the house. Above and below,
section and elevation drawings reveal the
regularity of the square-plan house.

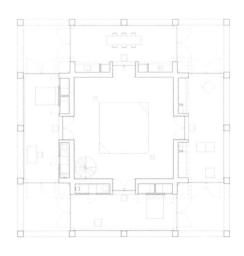

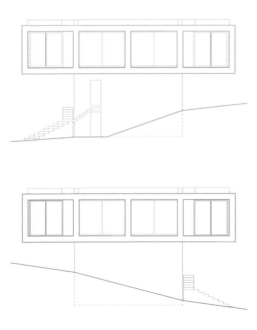

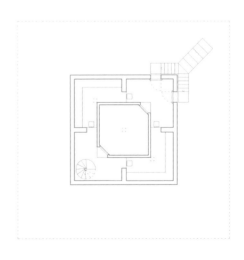

A panoramic perimeter ring punctuated by 16 columns
placed at regular intervals accommodates a sequence of
rooms with undefined functions.

Wiel Arets

V HOUSE

2013

LOCATION Maastricht, The Netherlands — **AREA** 530 m²
COLLABORATION Alex Kunnen, Jacques van Eyck, Breg Horemans

The name of this house is derived from Maastricht zoning rules that dictate that all new structures in the vicinity must remain within the envelope of preexisting buildings. The architects
explain that "a cut was created in the house's front façade to generate a triangulated surface,
which leads from one neighbor's sloped roof to the opposite neighbor's vertical bearing wall. As
the house's site is long and narrow, voids were cut into the maximum permitted volume to ensure
that natural light spills throughout the interior." A covered part of the ground floor is used to park
the owners' collection of Aston Martins. Sliding glass doors designed to admit the cars mark the
entry but, due to safety and privacy concerns, have no handles or keyholes and are, instead, re-
motely opened by an iPhone, from anywhere in the world. The poured-in-place concrete V House
is organized around its circulation paths as opposed to being set in a "stacked floor" scheme,
and is topped by a large roof terrace that offers panoramic views of Maastricht. A living room is
suspended from two I-beams and the kitchen and storage spaces were custom-designed.

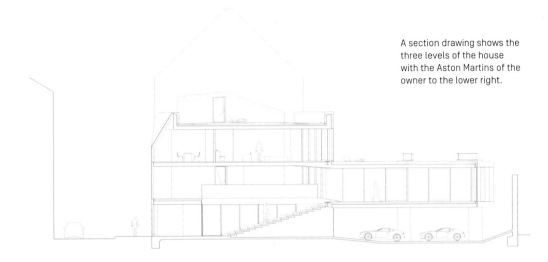

A section drawing shows the three levels of the house with the Aston Martins of the owner to the lower right.

←

The house stands out in a row of otherwise quite traditional Maastricht houses.

↑
Even from the relatively flat
rooftop, the house contrasts with
the neighborhood.

↓
The custom-designed kitchen and a glass,
steel, and concrete corner also differs from the
neighboring brick structures.

VILA ASPICUELTA

2012–13

LOCATION Rua Aspicuelta, São Paulo, SP, Brazil
AREA 590 m² — **CLIENT** Aphins Incorporação Imobiliária

The Vila Aspicuelta is a group of eight residences in the Vila Madalena neighborhood of São Paulo. The eight units are disposed side by side horizontally, but function vertically, and had to correspond to the precise zoning and dimensions pertaining to a new "village" in São Paulo.

Partially covered by the building, a street runs through the complex and gives access to the staircase of each unit. The parking lot, gardens, and common areas are also placed on this street. On the first floor of every house, one area is reserved for the kitchen, dining room, and living room. The second floor serves as a private area with a bedroom and balcony with a garden and bathroom. An open-air plaza is situated on the roof, with individual spaces for each unit, and the eastern orientation of the villa allows the houses to enjoy sunlit mornings, shady afternoons, and cross-ventilation. The western façade houses the access stairs of the units, and unifies the complex. The main construction materials are concrete, glass, aluminum, and wood.

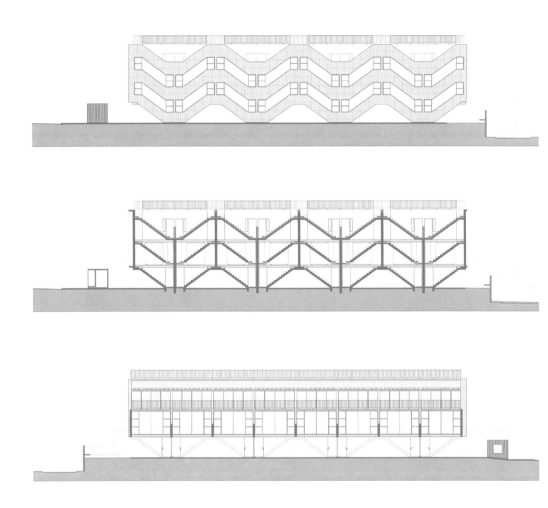

Section drawings show the building from
every angle with its undulating form resting
on four main supports.

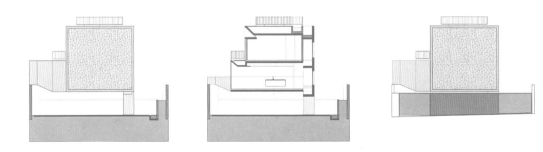

The architects deftly play on a contrast between opaque
and more transparent surfaces. The apparent weight of the
concrete is obviated by its floating appearance (below).

VILLA KABRU/CASA BRASIL III

2013

LOCATION Itacaré, Bahia, Brazil
AREA 180 m² — **CLIENT** Daniela Karagi, Patrick Armbruster

This residence is located on the outskirts of Itacaré, in the south of the state of Bahia, in the Atlantic Forest [Mata Atlantîca], which is a UNESCO World Cultural Heritage site. Built on a system of triangular platforms, it gives a "palpable sense of 360 degrees of openness," according to the architects. Available for rental, the house has an open-fronted living space with kitchen, several terraces, an open living platform, and a bedroom with a walk-in closet, and

the platforms are as high as six meters above the forest floor. In describing the building process the architects say that "a rough construction manual was drafted, based on a virtual 3-D model, and then put into action on the site itself by local tradesmen, without the aid of classic construction plans." Recycled wood from demolition sites and locally available materials were employed.

The atmosphere of a tree house or an open jungle
is maintained throughout the design, taking
into account the year-round average high tempera-
ture of 30° centigrade.

↑
A plan of the house shows a composition of superimposed triangles, a pattern that is prolonged even outside, as seen in the photo on the left page (bottom).

↓
The kitchen space is partially open like most of the rest of the structure. Here, the wooden frame stands out as a kind of light protection for the semi-internal spaces.

COM MERC IAL & PUB LIC

DOHA TOWER by JEAN NOUVEL

3XN

A–LAB

COOP HIMMELB(L)AU

SOU FUJIMOTO

MASSIMILIANO AND DORIANA FUKSAS

RICHARD MEIER

RYUE NISHIZAWA

JEAN NOUVEL

OMA

TRIPTYQUE

DALIAN INTERNATIONAL CONFERENCE CENTER

2008–12

LOCATION 116011 Zhongshan, Dalian, China — **AREA** 91 250 m² (Conference Center), 24 400 m² (parking) — **CLIENT** Dalian Municipal People's Government — **COST** €200 million

The rapidly developing city of Dalian is a major seaport located in the province of Liaoning in northeastern China. "The urban design task of the Dalian International Conference Center is to create an instantly recognizable landmark at the terminal point of the future extension of the main city axis," say the architects. Aside from the eight-floor Conference Center, which rises to a maximum height of 60 meters and occupies a 33 000-square-meter footprint, the complex contains a Theater and Opera House and an Exhibition Center. The architects go on to explain that "the structural concept is based on a sandwich structure composed of two elements: the 'table' and the roof. Both elements are steel space frames with depths ranging between 5 and 8 meters. The whole structure is elevated 7 meters above ground level and is supported by 14 vertical composite steel and concrete cores. A doubly ruled façade structure connects the two layers of table and roof, creating a load-bearing shell structure." Energy consumption is reduced through use of seawater for thermal control as well as natural ventilation and maximal natural lighting.

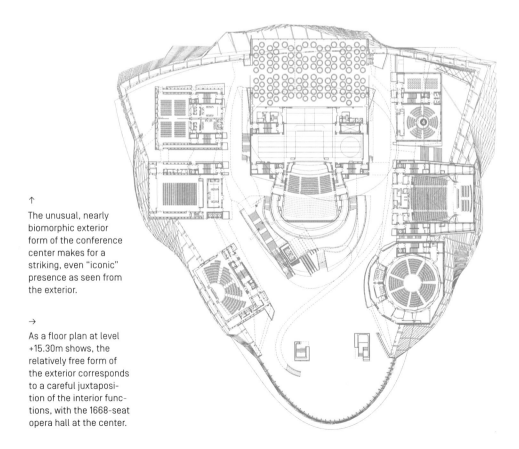

↑
The unusual, nearly biomorphic exterior form of the conference center makes for a striking, even "iconic" presence as seen from the exterior.

→
As a floor plan at level +15.30m shows, the relatively free form of the exterior corresponds to a careful juxtaposition of the interior functions, with the 1668-seat opera hall at the center.

↑
A foyer space reveals different interior levels but above all contributes to the architectural continuity of the design, where curves and slopes are an integral part of the concept.

↓
Wall and ceiling cladding in a conference room also participate in the studied overall design, where a sense of movement seems to always be in evidence.

DE ROTTERDAM

2009–13

LOCATION former harbor waterfront between KPN Tower and Cruise Terminal at Kop van Zuid, Rotterdam, The Netherlands, www.derotterdam.nl/en — **AREA** 162 000 m² — **CLIENT** De Rotterdam CV, The Hague — **COLLABORATION** Kees van Casteren (Associate in Charge)

Described as a 150-meter-high "mixed-use vertical city," this project is located on the former harbor waterfront between KPN Tower and Cruise Terminal at Kop van Zuid, and is the largest building in the Netherlands. Initially commissioned in 1997, the complex includes three interconnected towers housing offices (72 000 m²); 240 apartments (345 000 m²); a hotel (278 rooms) / congress / restaurant (19 000 m²); retail / food and beverage (1000 m²); leisure (4500 m²); and parking for 650 vehicles (31 000 m²). The different aspects of the program are divided into distinct blocks, though contact between all users occurs in the waterfront cafés. In the architects' words: "Urban density and diversity—both in the program and the form—are the guiding principles of the project. De Rotterdam's stacked towers are arranged in a subtly irregular cluster that refuses to resolve into a singular form and produces intriguing new views from different perspectives. Similarly, the definition of the building changes according to its multiple uses internally."

The design projects a sense of rigor both when seen from interiors but also in the more distant views of the triple tower (previous spread), which sits at the water's edge along the Nieuwe Maas opposite the main part of the city.

↓

A section drawing gives some sense of the size of the complex, and of the ways in which the architects have broken up the project to give a somewhat less massive appearance to the whole.

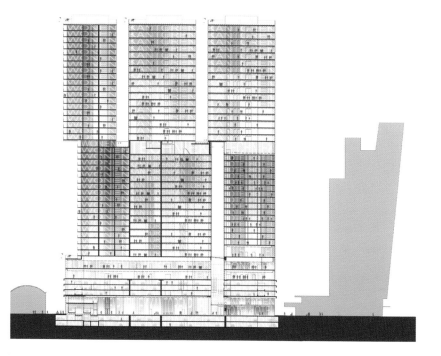

Jean Nouvel

DOHA TOWER

2007–13

ADRESS Al Corniche Street, West Bay, Doha, Qatar — **AREA** 60 000 m²
CLIENT Sheikh Saud Al Thani

The 231-meter-high Doha Tower has a cylindrical plan measuring 45 meters in diameter and is located in the center of the downtown area of Doha, which is called West Bay. There are 41 stories of rental office space and each floor provides panoramic views toward the Gulf, the Bay, the dense urban perspective of West Bay, or even the desert, according to orientation. The client has reserved the uppermost two stories of the tower for his own use. The building has an unusual entrance—with a sloping, landscaped ramp leading down to the main entrances that are below grade and covered by a circular canopy: landscape design is by Jean-Claude Hardy and takes into account the desert climate. As seen from street level, the building in fact appears to have no entrance—it becomes a purely sculptural object on the skyline, showing no visible surfaces in glass thanks to its unusual skin, formed with four "butterfly" aluminum elements of different scales, which are superimposed to create different densities according to orientation vis-à-vis the sun: 25% toward the north, 40% toward the south, and 60% on the east and west. Inside, a slightly reflective glass provides further protection, complemented by roller blinds where necessary. This combined system substantially reduces solar gain. Instead, the nighttime presence of the Doha Tower is enhanced by a computer-controlled LED system designed specifically for the façade by Yann Kersalé. During the design process, the Doha Tower showed a formal relation to two earlier projects by Jean Nouvel, the unbuilt Tour Sans Fins (Paris, 1989) and the Torre Agbar on the Avenida Diagonal in Barcelona (2000).

←
A view of the façade of the tower with its distinctive web of the "butterfly" aluminum panels, whose inspiration can be found in the typical geometric design of the *mashrabiya*.

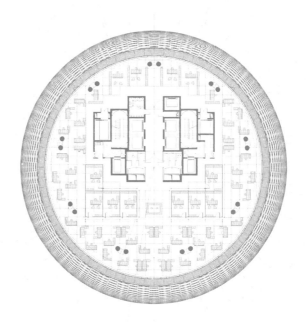

→
Two floor plans of the cylindrical complex also give some sense of being related to the elaborate geometric designs often seen in Islamic art. The lower drawing represents Jean Nouvel's proposal for level 44, a VIP area reserved for the client of the tower.

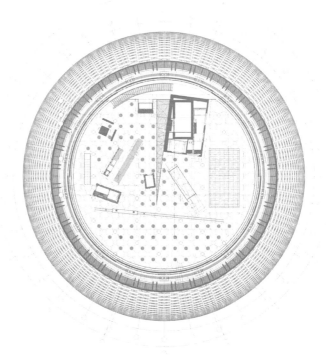

←

The entrance lobby level of the tower is actually below grade. The weight of the building is clearly born around the periphery by powerful V-shaped columns.

↓

Below are two images of the topmost VIP level of the tower before its full interior finishings had been put in place.

Ryue Nishizawa

FUKITA PAVILION IN SHODOSHIMA

2013

LOCATION Fukuda 598–1, Shodoshima, Kagawa, Japan
AREA 185 m^2 — CLIENT Shodoshima Town Office — COLLABORATION Mitsuhiro Kanada
(Structural Engineer, Arup Japan)

This unusual structure is a pavilion for a restaurant located on the premises of a shrine, next to the gymnasium of the Fukuda Elementary School in Shodoshima, an island in the Seto Inland Sea of Japan. It is comprised of two overlapping, curved sheets of steel, the corners of which are welded together, while the steel plate that forms the floor is prevented from flattening by the plate that serves as the roof. In turn, the roof plate is supported by the steel floor as it slightly "slouches" in the center. The space thus created between the two sheets of metal provides seating for visitors, and also serves as a playground for children in the area leading to the temple. Despite its rather ephemeral appearance, this is a permanent structure, although without any foundations. "It is a simple arrangement, as if the pavilion had just been brought along and placed there," the architects say.

Though it looks like it might be made of cloth, the pavilion is formed with steel sheets that seem to hang from the trees, almost without other visible means of support. The usual elements of architecture have been replaced by two curving plates of metal.

OSCAR FREIRE

2012–13

LOCATION Rua Oscar Freire 1128, Jardins São Paulo, SP, Brazil
AREA 675 m² — CLIENT Fernando Tchalian

The architects explain that this project was inspired by Yona Friedman's 1959 "Spatial City." Their solution consists in a small complex of three shops, one restaurant, a bar, and an art gallery. The floor level with the restaurant and stores is compared to the traditional city, while a "spatial" level contains a gallery or "observatory." The cubic observatory, clad in stainless steel, is "balanced on an asymmetric structure that imparts kinetic energy and operates a disruption between the street level and the 'space' effect," according to the architects. For Triptyque, "architecture is a dynamic form, between materiality and potentiality, open to user interaction as well as environmental conditions."

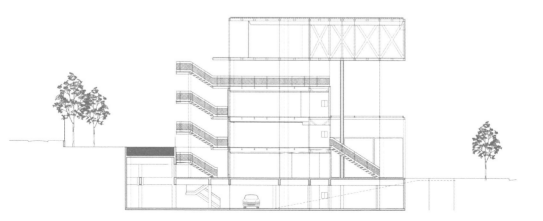

Yona Friedman stated that in a "mobile city" buildings should touch a minimum area on the ground, be able to be dismantled or moved, and be capable of being altered by individual occupants.

Sou Fujimoto

PUBLIC TOILET IN ICHIHARA

2012

LOCATION Itabu Station, Ichihara City, Chiba, Japan — **AREA** 209 m²
CLIENT Ichihara City — **COLLABORATION** Nao Harikae, Naganobu Matsumura, Naoki Tamura

Though a public toilet may not seem the most obvious place for a talented architect to challenge architectural suppositions, this is precisely what Sou Fujimoto sought to do in the case of the Public Toilet in Ichihara. Located near the Itabu Station on a local train line, this toilet consists of two units, one for women and the other which is "unisex and for people with disabilities." The area around the station is known for its scenery and in particular for the spring cherry blossoms, which posed certain design issues, as the ar-

chitect explains: "A public toilet is, in a way, the smallest public facility. It is public, and, at the same time, it is a very private space. Therefore, it is the usual premise to close and to protect the location from its surroundings. However, in the midst of this beautiful environment, the question is raised of how it can be closed while remaining open. And this closed-but-openedness challenges us to reflect on a primitive form of architecture." A wooden log fence is used to enclose an area of 209 square meters that contains the toilets in their natural environment. "This multilayered divergence of internal and external boundaries blends together public and private, the sense of openness and protection, nature and architecture, internal and external, large and small, while retaining their ambiguity," says Fujimoto.

SHENZHEN STOCK EXCHANGE

2008-13

LOCATION Fu Zhong 3 Road, Futian Central District, Shenzhen, China — **AREA** 265 000 m²
CLIENT Shenzhen Stock Exchange — **COLLABORATION** Michael Kokora (Associate in Charge)

This project is the first to have been completed in China by OMA after the CCTV building (Beijing, 2012). The three-story base of the Shenzhen Stock Exchange is cantilevered 36 meters above the ground, creating a large public space below and a roof garden above, and contains the listing hall and all stock exchange offices. Although it has a square form like many nearby structures, the building "is differentiated through its materiality: a translucent layer of patterned glass wraps the tower grid and raised podium, rendering the façade mysterious and enigmatic, while revealing the construction behind," according to the architects. Rem Koolhaas goes on to say that "the Shenzhen Stock Exchange embodies the Pearl River Delta's phenomenal transformation over the past 30 years. We are greatly excited about the building from an architectural standpoint, but I believe its true significance emerges when viewed in an economic, political, and ultimately social context." Construction was overseen by OMA Asia's Hong Kong office and the firm's on-site office in Shenzhen throughout the construction process. OMA's team consisted of over 75 architects at various points in the design and construction phases.

→

A section of the structure
where the Shenzhen Stock
Exchange offices are located
in the central tower, at the
level of the broad, cantilevered volume.

↓

The plan below shows the
eighth floor of the complex
where the stock listing
hall is located.

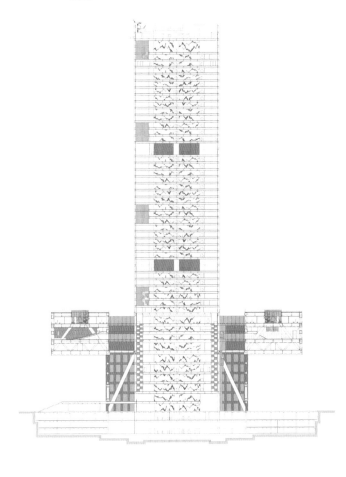

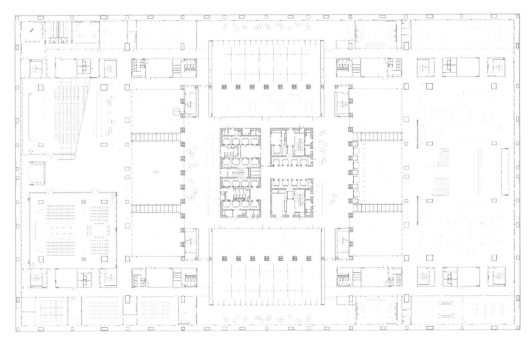

Two views of the unexpected rectangular
block that projects from the tower, with the one
below showing the rooftop podium garden.

STATOIL REGIONAL AND INTERNATIONAL OFFICES

2010–12

LOCATION Martin Linges vei 25, 1364 Fornebu, Norway, www.statoil.no
AREA 65 500 m² — **CLIENT** IT Property AS (owner) / Statoil ASA (tenant) — **COST** €200 million

The architects won an open competition in 2009 for the design and construction of this project. Statoil is a Norwegian energy producer, the 57th largest company in the world by revenue, with about 30 000 employees in 37 countries. 2500 people work in this office building, which occupies the former site of Oslo Airport, currently being developed, integrating its 52 000-square-meter parking lot. The structure consists of five office rectangles, stacked on top of each other, of identical size: 140 meters in length, 23 meters in width, and three stories in height. The orientation of each block is optimized for the use of natural light and for the views over adjacent

public park areas and the fjord of Oslo. Oil industry construction methods inspired the steel superstructure of the building and 1600 prefabricated elements make up the façade. A central atrium, used by all employees to access to their offices, is covered by a "propeller-shaped" glass roof. "The concept minimizes the environmental footprint of the building and gives a generous amount of space to the park," according to the architects, who emphasize the design's flexibility for future use and energy efficiency.

Although the basic volumes of the structure are strictly rectangular, their stacking and rotation gives an unexpected and dynamic appearance to the whole.

→

The underside of one of
the volumes is the location
of a commissioned artwork
by the noted Swiss artist
Pipilotti Rist. A combination
of colored, backlit canvas
and LED screens covers an
area of 1200 m².

↓

Apparently inspired by the
Mikado pick-up sticks game,
the seemingly random placement of the "lamellas" is re-
solved in a coherent, ordered
manner as the section drawing below demonstrates.

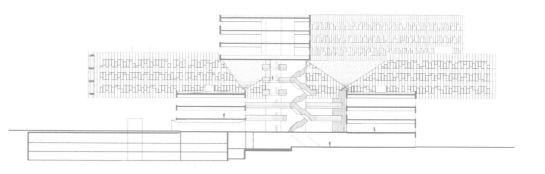

Interior spaces are marked by a number of commissioned artworks. The architects use the points where the rotated stacks intersect to create interstitial spaces with public areas.

TERMINAL 3

2010–13

LOCATION Shenzhen Bao'an International Airport, Shenzhen, China, +86 755 2345 6789, www.eng.szairport.com — **AREA** 500 000 m²
CLIENT Shenzhen Airport (Group) Co. Ltd. — **COST** €734 million
COLLABORATION Knippers Helbig Eng., Stuttgart; Speirs & Major Associates, Edinburgh, London

The design of this project evokes "the image of a manta ray, a fish that breathes and changes its own shape, undergoes variations, and turns into a bird to celebrate the emotion and fantasy of flight." Terminal 3's 1.5-kilometer-long tunnel-like structure is also compared by the architect to an "organic-shaped sculpture" with the roof profile referring to a natural landscape. The structure is enveloped in a double "internal and external" honeycomb-skin cladding made of alveola-shaped, partially operable metal and glass panels of different size that allows light in while protecting the interior space. Inside, the concourse is made up of three levels, each dedicated to an

This overall view of the facility empha-
sizes its organic or airplane-inspired form,
which is clearly related to the functions
of this major airport.

independent function: departures, arrivals, and services. A "cross" marks the intersection point
where the three levels of the concourse are vertically connected to create full-height voids,
allowing natural light to filter from the highest level down to the waiting room area in the node
of the ground-level square, which admits users to the luggage, departure, and arrivals areas, as
well as to coffee shops, restaurants, offices, and business facilities. Double- and triple-height
areas characterize the departure zone. The interiors were also designed by Fuksas, including the
check-in, security-check, gates, and passport-check areas.

The cross-like shape seen in the overall
plan below and in the image above marks the
point where the three levels of the terminal
communicate vertically.

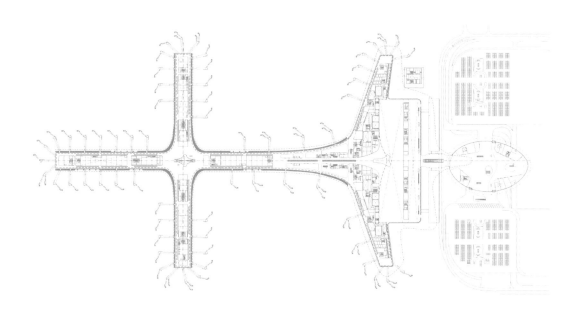

The sweeping design shares a great deal with the form
of airplanes, but the openings in its skin also give it an almost
reptilian appearance, as seen in the photo below. Above,
the roof curves over an entrance area.

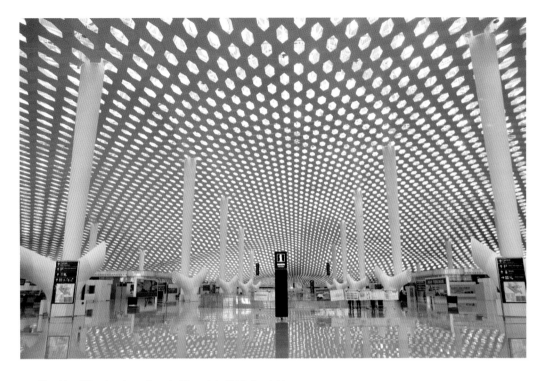

The skin of the structure allows in filtered daylight. Furnishings
and air ducts were also designed by the architects, allowing for an
exceptional degree of formal unity.

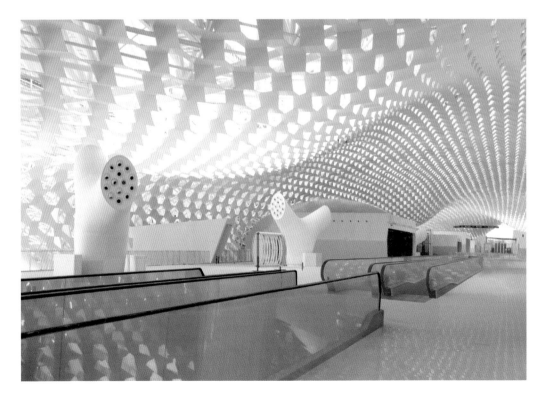

The repetitive nature of the ceiling openings is animated by the curves in the structure and the variable effects due to changing outdoor light. Fuksas has mastered the art of building architecturally inventive buildings on a very large scale.

UN CITY

2010–14

LOCATION Marmorvej 51, Marmormolen, 2100 Copenhagen, Denmark, www.un.dk/en
AREA 45 000 m² (office and public facilities); 7000 m² (archives and secondary facilities) — CLIENT By og Havn A/S — COST €134 million   COLLABORATION Gry Kjær, Peter Feltendal

Intended for the regional offices of the United Nations in Copenhagen, the architects explain that their "design is a response to the UN's wishes for an iconic building expressing the organization's values and authority." Set on an artificial island in the Marmormolen area of the city, the white building, covered by perforated aluminum shutters, rests on a dark steel base and forms an eight-pointed star. The three-meter-long shutters reduce solar gain without blocking daylight or views and can be controlled by employees from their own computers. A daylight-filled atrium with a central staircase connects the entrance lobby with the office areas. More than 1400 solar panels are set on the roof, and cold seawater is pumped into the cooling system, further reducing energy use. Designed to be one of Denmark's most energy efficient buildings, the structure has achieved a LEED Platinum certification and was awarded the GreenBuilding Award 2012 by the European Commission.

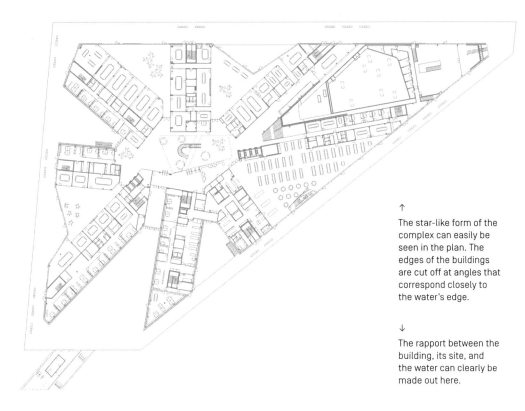

↑
The star-like form of the complex can easily be seen in the plan. The edges of the buildings are cut off at angles that correspond closely to the water's edge.

↓
The rapport between the building, its site, and the water can clearly be made out here.

→

The architects have varied cladding materials, window sizes, and the angles of the structures to provide relief from the monotony that could be a problem for such a large project.

↓

Convivial outdoor spaces, such as the wooden terrace, are also part of the scheme that aims to encourage sociable work circumstances.

Richard Meier

UNITED STATES COURTHOUSE

2003–13

LOCATION 333 West Broadway, San Diego, CA 92101, USA, +1 619 557 6620
AREA 43 082 m² — **CLIENT** United States General Services Administration — **COST** $382 million
COLLABORATION Michael Palladino, James Crawford

The new United states Courthouse includes a slender 16-story tower, clad in thin layers of terra-cotta and glass rising above a transparent base, while the glass-roofed lobby is elliptical in form and has numerous mezzanines. Natural light, even in the courtroom areas, is a priority, as is color. In the words of the architects: "The palette of materials and 'color' of the new courthouse are inspired by the city itself and its Mediterranean quality of place. The warm off-whites that turn golden at sunset help set the Mediterranean stage that makes San Diego unique. To achieve this color, façade materials include natural stone, terracotta, precast concrete, and cast-in-place concrete." The project's design incorporates principles of sustainability and energy efficiency that allowed it to receive a LEED Gold certification. In addition to the courthouse, the master plan for this project integrates new and existing federal buildings with gardens, plazas, a water feature, and pedestrian paths that engage downtown urban design goals.

Balconies and glazed passageways offer views of the city in a type of structure that might be expected to be more closed. A ground level view shows that the structure fits into its environment, but also stands out with its clean, carefully designed lines and materials.

← \
Light-filled atrium spaces are a frequent feature of Richard Meier's public buildings and the United States Courthouse is no exception.

↓ \
A floor plan of the rectangular building shows the ordered complexity of its interior, here that of typical courtrooms.

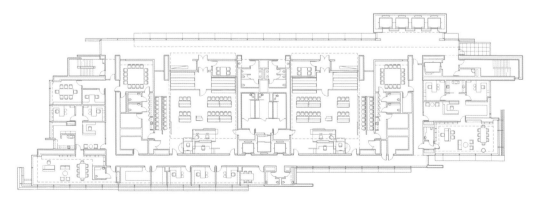

CUL TURE & RELIG ION

HEYDAR ALIYEV CENTER by ZAHA HADID

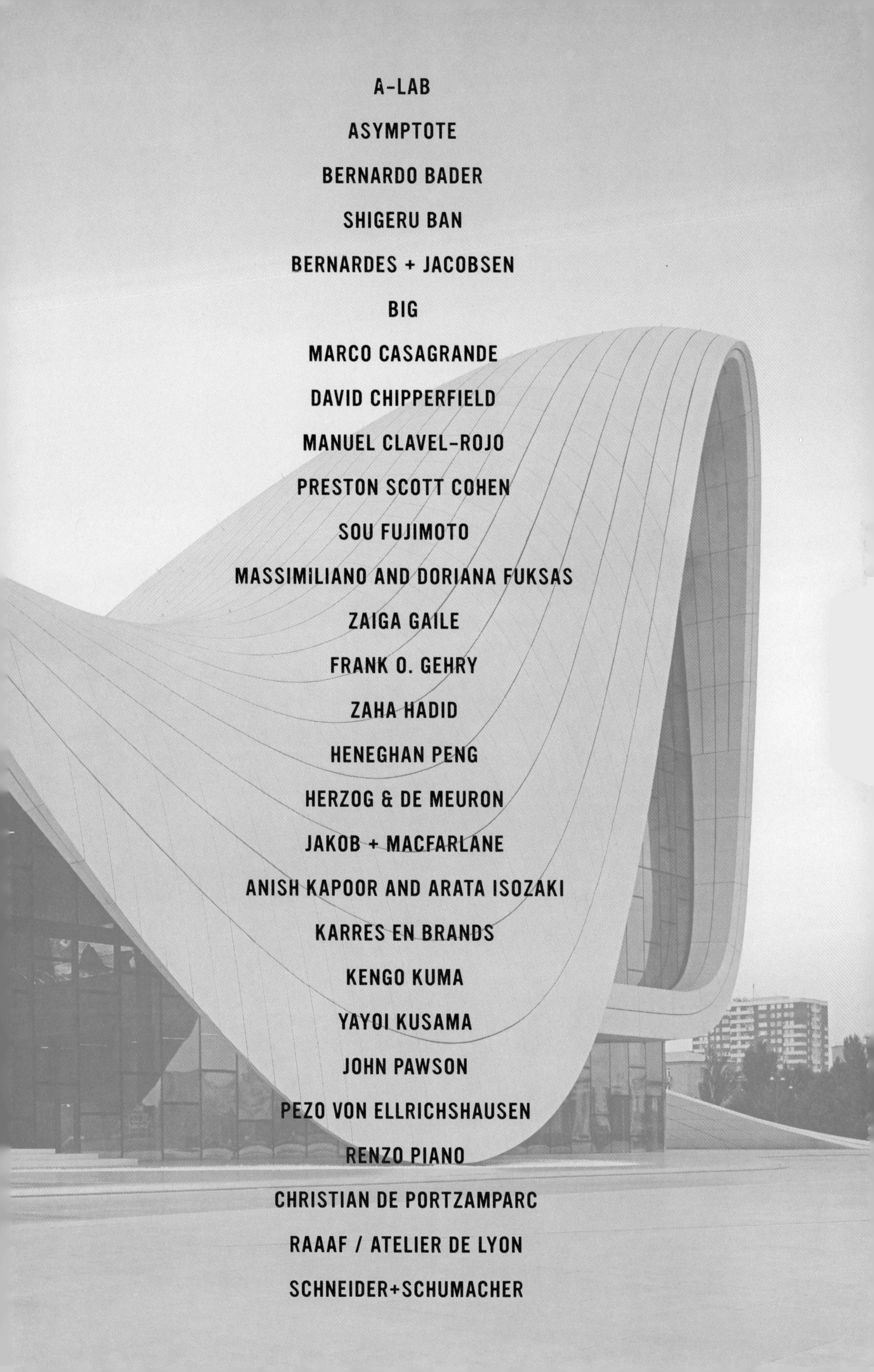

A-LAB

ASYMPTOTE

BERNARDO BADER

SHIGERU BAN

BERNARDES + JACOBSEN

BIG

MARCO CASAGRANDE

DAVID CHIPPERFIELD

MANUEL CLAVEL-ROJO

PRESTON SCOTT COHEN

SOU FUJIMOTO

MASSIMILIANO AND DORIANA FUKSAS

ZAIGA GAILE

FRANK O. GEHRY

ZAHA HADID

HENEGHAN PENG

HERZOG & DE MEURON

JAKOB + MACFARLANE

ANISH KAPOOR AND ARATA ISOZAKI

KARRES EN BRANDS

KENGO KUMA

YAYOI KUSAMA

JOHN PAWSON

PEZO VON ELLRICHSHAUSEN

RENZO PIANO

CHRISTIAN DE PORTZAMPARC

RAAAF / ATELIER DE LYON

SCHNEIDER+SCHUMACHER

a-lab

AKS—ARCTIC CULTURAL CENTER

2004–08

LOCATION Strandgata 30, 9600 Hammerfest, Norway, +47 78 40 20 99, www.aks.no
AREA 5000 m² — **CLIENT** Municipality of Hammerfest — **COST** €22 million

Hammerfest presents itself as the world's northernmost city, and receives over 250 000 visitors a year. Part of a larger seafront development, the Arctic Cultural Center is visible from both land and sea. Used for art events, cultural activities, and conferences, it was the first structure on the so-called Findus site and, as such, has encouraged further development in the area and opened the center of the city toward the sea. Public areas are maximized between the compact units that house the program, linking the Center to the rest of the city, with the foyer area—in the words of the architects—"formalized as a public climate-controlled open space between built masses, connecting the main coastal road [Strandgata] to the quay along the waterline three meters below." The "Arctic Arena" is another open, outdoor space. The structural system consists of a steel framework with reinforced-concrete walls and the façades are made with laminated wood with aluminum-framed windows and glass that is lit with an LED system.

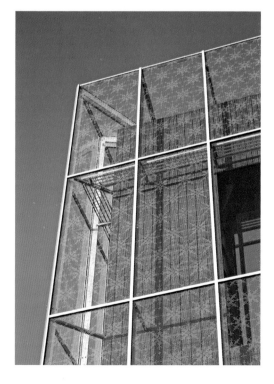

Supported partially by tilted pilotis,
the structure appears to sit lightly on
its site despite an orthogonal form.

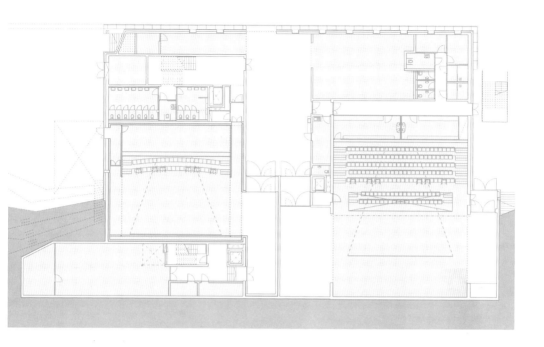

↑
A plan with the main auditorium on the right.
The blackbox/cinema is on the left.

↓
Interior views of the complex with its large
glass façade facing the water.

Pezo von Ellrichshausen

"BLUE PAVILION"

2014

LOCATION Royal Academy of Arts, London, UK — **AREA** 152 m²
CLIENT Royal Academy of Arts

This realization was part of the exhibition "Sensing Spaces: Architecture Reimagined," held at the Royal Academy of Arts in London from January 25 to April 6, 2014. The three-story structure was made with untreated pine boards and consisted of a small, square, elevated room supported by four massive round columns. The room was left open to the decorated ceiling of the gallery, while four hollowed columns contained spiral staircases that gave direct access to the upper platform, which could also be reached via a compact ramp. The architects illustrate the project in these words: "As a whole, the piece can be understood as an enigmatic device that invites visitors to abandon the normal stratum of the exhibition space to inhabit its vertical dimension." The "Blue Pavilion" was assembled at the Royal Academy by the four carpenters who prefabricated its pieces in Chile.

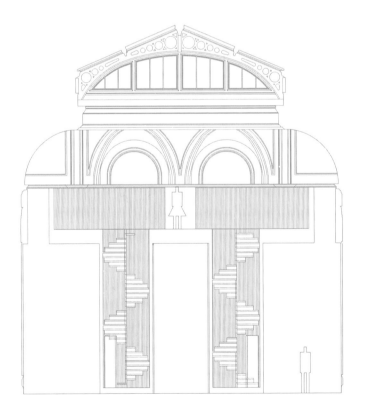

↑
Visitors were encouraged to climb up into the structure and to view the details of the ceiling of the Royal Academy gallery.

←
A transversal section through the platform shows the scale of visitors.

Visitors were offered the possibility to
go up through spiral staircases (top) or up
a long wooden ramp.

BUNKER 599

2010

LOCATION Diefdijk 5, Zijderveld, The Netherlands — **AREA** 30 m²
CLIENT DLG (Dutch Service for Land and Water Management)

Bunker 599 forms part of the New Dutch Waterline (NDW), a military line of defense in use from 1815 until 1940, which protected the cities of Muiden, Utrecht, Vreeswijk, and Gorinchem by means of intentional flooding. The designers explain: "A seemingly indestructible bunker with monumental status is sliced open. The design thereby opens up the minuscule interior of one of NDW's 700 bunkers, the insides of which are normally cut off from view completely. In addition, a long wooden boardwalk cuts through the extremely heavy construction leading visitors to a flooded area and to the footpaths of the adjacent natural reserve." Also visible from the main A2 highway, Bunker 599 aims to make an unexpected part of Dutch history accessible and tangible for visitors.

CARDBOARD CATHEDRAL

2013

LOCATION 234 Hereford Street, Christchurch Central, Christchurch 8011, New Zealand, +64 3 366 0046, www.cardboardcathedral.org.nz — **AREA** 770 m² — **CLIENT** Christchurch Cathedral **COLLABORATION** Yoshie Narimatsu (Shigeru Ban Architects), Peter Marshall, Eugene Coleman (Warren & Mahoney)

During the February 22, 2011 earthquake, 185 people were killed and more than 80% of buildings in central Christchurch were either destroyed or damaged beyond repair. The cathedral in the square was severely damaged, with its spire collapsing. Plans were made as of May 2011 to create a "transitional" cathedral in its place. Working as he has on other disaster relief projects on a pro bono basis (free of charge), Shigeru Ban created the transitional Cardboard Cathedral near the Canterbury Television site, where 115 people—including 13 Japanese students—died in 2011. Made with timber, paper tubes, polycarbonate sheeting, and ceramic printed glass, the tent-like structure certainly assumes the role of the cathedral with grace. Its materials confer a certain modesty that is befitting of its religious function and in a sense typical of the architect.

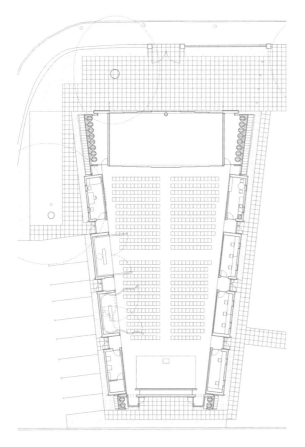

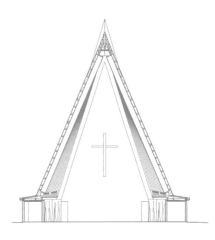

↑

The interior of the cathedral with its chairs designed by the architect and his signature cardboard tube elements used in structural or decorative aspects of the design.

←

A floor plan with Hereford Street at the top.

↓

A short section drawing with the main cross of the cathedral.

Shigeru Ban designed not only the architecture of the cathedral, but also its furnishings, including liturgical elements as seen above (left).

Christian de Portzamparc

CIDADE DAS ARTES

2004–13

LOCATION Av. das Américas 5300, Barra da Tijuca, RJ 22793–080, Brazil, +55 21 3325 0102, www.cidadedasartes.org — AREA 46 000 m² — CLIENT City of Rio de Janeiro, Secretaria Municipal das Culturas — COLLABORATION Bertrand Beau, Clovis Cunha, Nanda Eskes (Assistant Architects)

The Cidade das Artes forms a single large structure with a vast terrace set 10 meters above ground level at the crossing of Americas and Ayrton Senna avenues, originally designed by Lúcio Costa in the Barra da Tijuca area of the city. Intended for chamber music (500 seats) as well as popular music, three movie theaters, dance studios, 10 rehearsal rooms, exhibition spaces, restaurants, and a media library, the design is characterized by the two horizontal plates that form the roof and the main terrace. Between these two horizontal limits, curved concrete walls contain the halls and establish an interplay of solids and voids. The 1800-seat Philharmonic Hall can be converted into a 1300-seat Opera. The architect describes this work as a "public symbol" and a landmark for a new area of Rio.

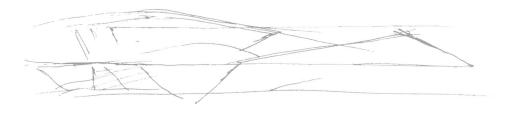

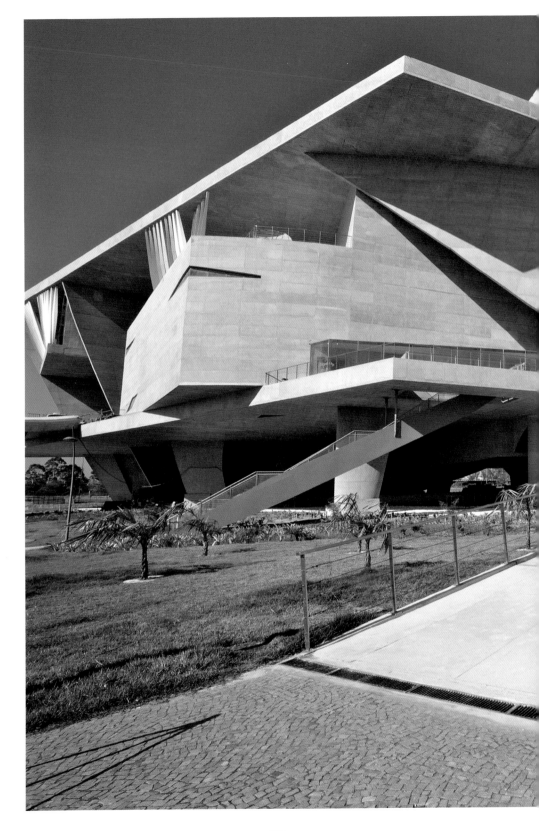

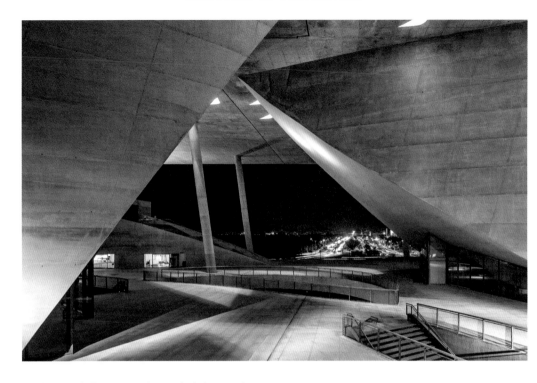

Christian de Portzamparc has made daring use of
concrete in this project, partially as an indirect homage
to the great Brazilian architect Oscar Niemeyer.

 ↑
As he did in the Cité de la
Musique in Paris, Christian de
Portzamparc creates open pas-
sages within the building that
are like urban streets, giving a
sense of the substantial dimensions of the project.

→
The main concert hall of the
Cidade das Artes was also
designed by the architect.

Manuel Clavel-Rojo

CLOUD PANTHEON

2010

LOCATION cemetery in Espinardo, Murcia, Spain — **AREA** 53 m²
COLLABORATION Robin Harloff, Mauricio Méndez-Bustos, David Hernández-Conesa

The project concerned "a stage setting for a burial, taking into account the spatial and temporal situations" with the interior inspired by "a cloud that is crossed by beams of sun." The large abstract cloud was made with triangulated steel plates coated in white polyurethane paint. The rear wall is translucent allowing in minimal natural light, while three irregular skylights admit more daylight and give the "cloud" a "weightless and enigmatic" appearance. Five trapezoidal doors made of tinted glass are framed in satin-finished stainless steel; revolving on hidden metallic rods, they appear to be permanently closed. The difference in pavement between the levels that are above and below ground is intended to "symbolize the transition from one world to another." Black basalt is used below, and white Macael marble above grade.

COLUMBARIUM - DEEL 4

DE NIEUWE OOSTER CEMETERY

2005–

LOCATION Kruislaan 126, 1097 GA Amsterdam, The Netherlands,
+31 20 608 06 08, www.denieuweooster.nl — AREA 1 ha (burial field); 33 ha (total cemetery area)
CLIENT De Nieuwe Ooster COST €820 000 (columbarium)

Built in 2007–08, the columbarium (a place for storing funeral urns) was designed as a component of the Crematorium Garden of Remembrance and is part of an ongoing program of work by the architects at the Nieuwe Ooster Cemetery in Amsterdam. Covering a floor area of 625 square meters, the 120-meter-long, 5-meter-wide, and 5-meter-high volume is cut by pathways and provides space for 1000 urns in "hollowed out" rooms. It looks like "an introverted and robust zinc sculpture," according to the architects. Interior rooms have white terrazzo walls with a pattern of single and double niches hollowed out of the walls. Openings in the wall allow views of the surroundings, and most spaces enclosed by walls are open to the sky.

↑
Drawings show the some-
what irregular forms of the
burial area walls.

↓
An image taken
within the enclosure of
the cemetery walls.

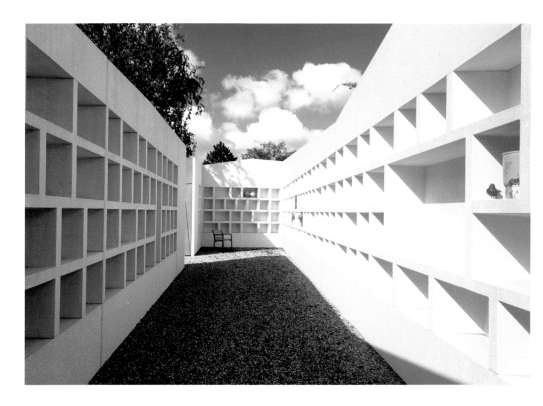

→

The cemetery gives a large place to the natural setting or to features such as this pond. The overall impression is one of peace.

↓

The organization of the grounds makes future expansion possible, all the while maintaining a clear sense of human scale and as much privacy as possible.

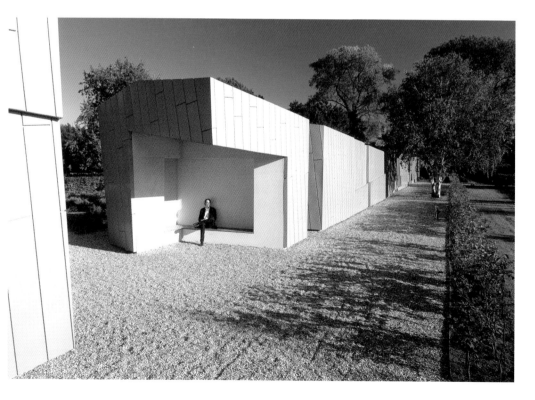

Kengo Kuma

FRAC PACA

2011–13

LOCATION 20 Boulevard de Dunkerque, 13002 Marseille, France, +33 4 91 91 27 55, www.fracpaca.org — **AREA** 8048 m² — **CLIENT** Région Provence Alpes Côte d'Azur, AREA — **COST** €21.5 million — **COLLABORATION** Toury Vallet (Associate Architect)

The architect describes this project as a three-dimensional version of André Malraux's "museum without walls." The clear intention of those involved was to create a symbol in the city meant to increase the visibility of contemporary art and to encourage active connections between the city and the FRAC PACA, through emphasizing the openness of the building and its permanent connection with the exterior. Made up of two distinct parts, the main section, running along Rue Vincent Leblanc, includes the exhibition space and offices, while the tower includes a café, auditorium, and teaching atelier, and offers a view along Boulevard de Dunkerque. The façade is made with laminated tempered glass and enamel paint, as well as fiber-cement panels and galvanized metal. The outdoor sculpture garden was created in association with the Lycée des Calanques, a local high school specialized in landscape design.

The cladding of the tower block gives a distinct
impression of permeability or openness. Inside, spaces
are flexible and generous in size and area.

Heneghan Peng

GIANT'S CAUSEWAY VISITOR CENTER

2010-12

LOCATION 44 Causeway Road, Bushmills, County Antrim BT57 8SU, UK,
+44 28 2073 1855, www.nationaltrust.org.uk/giants-causeway — AREA 1800 m²
CLIENT National Trust — COST €11.16 million

The Visitor Center is the gateway to the Giant's Causeway, a group of approximately 40 000 interlocking basalt columns that are the result of an ancient volcanic eruption, to be found on the North Antrim coast in Northern Ireland. The Giant's Causeway is a UNESCO World Heritage Site, which imposes particular care on the design of any new building, as the architects readily acknowledged: "The proposal for the new visitor facilities can be understood as two folds into the landscape. One folds upwards revealing the building and the second folds down to form

The use of basalt for exterior faces is certainly an echo of the unusual natural site concerned, but no sense of what might be called geomorphic imitation is in evidence.

the car park and shield it from view of the approach road and coastal path. Between the two folds, a ramp leads to the coastal ridgeline that is restored at this location." The external faces of the building are in basalt, glazing, and stainless steel, while poured-in-place concrete, basalt, glazing, stainless steel, anodized aluminum, oak, and polished concrete are employed on the interiors. Inside, a series of stepping floor plates are linked by a sequence of ramps and a café is set near the main entrance with a view of the coastline.

The Visitor Center makes a point of being discreet
and bows not only to the natural setting, but also to
nearby older buildings.

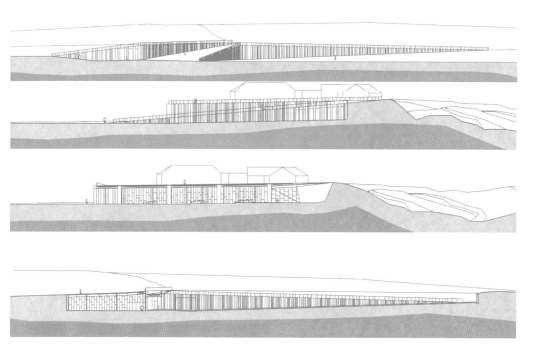

The interiors have a decidedly mineral aspect that is appropriate to the site. Polished concrete and basalt alternate with the high glazing that allows in sufficient natural light.

↑
Elevation and section drawings show the long, low profile of the building, as well as its insertion into the topography of the site.

HEYDAR ALIYEV CENTER

2012

LOCATION 1 Heydar Aliyev prospekti, Baku AZ1033, Azerbaijan, +994 12 505 60 01, www.heydaraliyevcenter.az/#main — AREA 101 801 m² — CLIENT Republic of Azerbaijan

Since its independence in 1991, Azerbaijan has invested heavily in modernizing and developing Baku's infrastructure and architecture. Zaha Hadid Architects were appointed design architects of the Heydar Aliyev Center—intended as the main showcase for the country's cultural programs—as a result of a 2007 competition. Built on a site that incorporates an existing sheer drop, the structure seeks to achieve an appearance of continuity and homogeneity as its design "establishes a continuous, fluid relationship between its surrounding plaza and the building's interior," perhaps inspired, as Hadid points out, by "Muslim designs that often celebrated fluidity in architecture and in the decorative arts." The plaza envelops public interior space that willfully promotes both traditional and contemporary Azeri culture. The concrete space frame structure of the building is combined with vertical structural elements absorbed by the envelope and curtain wall. Glass Fiber Reinforced Concrete (GFRC) and Glass Fiber Reinforced Polyester (GFRP) were chosen as cladding materials, and careful attention was paid to the overall lighting scheme.

↑
The profile of the building seems to surge up from the mineral surroundings; indeed its lines are continued into the square and the broader site.

The wavelike forms of the building are not specifically biomorphic, and yet they do appear to have a "natural" origin—in any case, the architect's predilection for sweeping curves here finds its apotheosis.

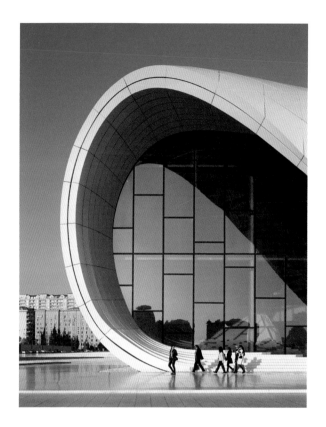

The outer curves of the structure give an impression of architecture unlike any other. The building does not necessarily express its own function, but appears rather to be a self-evident result of the program and the site.

→

Even in the auditorium, which seats 1000 people, the overall concept of spatial fluidity and continuity is maintained with the curved alignment of the seats seeming to form the very shape of the hall.

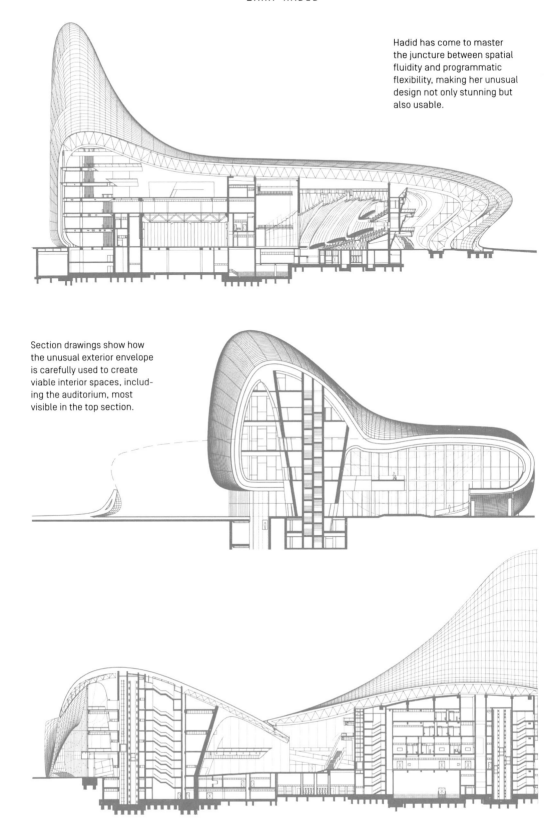

Hadid has come to master the juncture between spatial fluidity and programmatic flexibility, making her unusual design not only stunning but also usable.

Section drawings show how the unusual exterior envelope is carefully used to create viable interior spaces, including the auditorium, most visible in the top section.

Interior volumes echo the spectacular curves of the exterior of the building, sometimes allowing floors to sweep upward to become ceilings or to wrap into stairways or balconies (below).

"INFINITY MIRRORED ROOM –
THE SOULS OF MILLIONS OF LIGHT YEARS AWAY"
& "LOVE IS CALLING"

2013

Overall dimensions for "Infinity Mirrored Room" 288 × 415 × 415 cm
Overall dimensions for "Love Is Calling" 443 × 865 × 608 cm

Both of these works were presented in the solo exhibition "I Who Have Arrived in Heaven" at David Zwirner in New York (November 8–December 21, 2013). "Infinity Mirrored Room" is a cube-shaped, mirror-paneled room with a shallow reflecting pool as its floor. Hundreds of multicolored LED lights are suspended at varying heights from the ceiling, flickering off and on. The repetitive pattern of illumination and reflections produced is meant to suggest endlessness and ultimately invoke concepts of life and death. The work is made of wood, metal, glass mirrors, plastic, acrylic panel, rubber, an LED lighting system, acrylic balls, and water. "Love Is Calling" is an immersive, kaleidoscopic environment. It is composed of a darkened, mirrored room illuminated by inflatable, tentacle-like forms extending from floor to ceiling and covered in the artist's characteristic polka dots. A sound recording of Kusama reciting a love poem in Japanese plays continuously.

Bernardo Bader

ISLAMIC CEMETERY

2010–11

LOCATION Schotterried 1, 6844 Altach, Austria (L 190 Hohenems/Götzis)
AREA 468 m² — **CLIENT** Municipality of Altach — **COST** $2.98 million
COLLABORATION Azra Akšamija (Art), Eva Grabherr (Consulting)

Religious burials have only recently become possible for Muslims—accounting for more than 10% of the local population—in Vorarlberg, western Austria, whence the construction of this Islamic Cemetery. The architects won an invited competition in 2006 for the complex, constructed in reinforced concrete, with oak used on the entrance façade and for a large wooden screen with Islamic geometric patterns that defines spaces in the indoor prayer area. A "partially roofed space large enough to accommodate the congregation and a crowd of mourners opens onto the courtyard and is characterized by a lively play of light and shadow," according to the architects, and openings attentively frame views of the burial garden and Bregenz Forest in the distance. Outside, five burial areas are marked by red concrete walls designed in a lattice pattern that further connects the spaces to the natural setting, affirming the architect's idea of the cemetery as a "primordial garden." The citation for the Aga Khan Award for Architecture, received by the project in 2013, reads in part: "Simple in expression and poetic in form, it not only engages the natural landscape in an intelligent manner but also suspends any notion of declaration. While emphasizing spiritual pluralism, the cemetery also provides the final destination for a minority group in a dominant society."

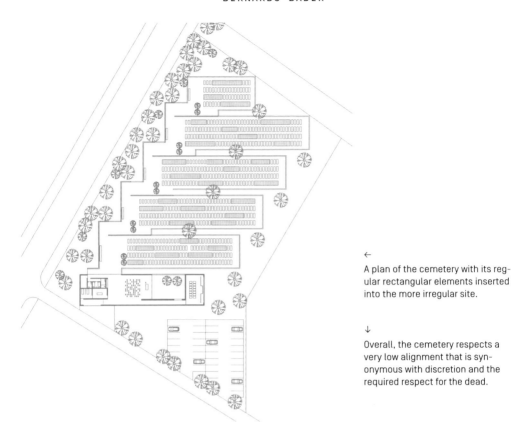

←

A plan of the cemetery with its reg-ular rectangular elements inserted into the more irregular site.

↓

Overall, the cemetery respects a very low alignment that is syn-onymous with discretion and the required respect for the dead.

Enclosed spaces also adapt a minimalist vocabulary
with a geometric clarity that inhabits spaces, like the outdoor courtyard above, or the prayer space below.

KIMBELL ART MUSEUM EXPANSION

2010–13

LOCATION 3333 Camp Bowie Boulevard, Fort Worth, TX 76107–2792, USA, +1 817 332 8451, www.kimbellart.org — **AREA** 9395 m² — **CLIENT** Kimbell Art Foundation — **COST** $135 million

Recognized as one of the masterpieces of modern architecture, Louis Kahn's 1972 Kimbell Art Museum near downtown Fort Worth posed a particular challenge to Renzo Piano and his team. The so-called Piano Pavilion has a floor area of 9395 square meters as opposed to the 11 148 square meters of the original Kahn building and adds 1505 square meters of gallery space, an education center, auditorium, and library, as well as parking space. Alabaster-toned architectural concrete, laminated Douglas-fir ceiling beams, and quarter-sawn, engineered, white-oak flooring are the main visible materials, together with triple-glazed, gas-filled glass. The architects explain: "Echoing Kahn's building in height, scale, and general layout, the RPBW building has a more open, transparent character." A green roof, photovoltaic cells, geothermal wells, and low-energy LED lighting contribute to the overall energy efficiency of the new building. The Kimbell Art Museum is located across the street from Tadao Ando's Modern Art Museum of Fort Worth (2002).

Renzo Piano met the challenge of creating new spaces that somehow echo the nearly mythical interiors of the original Louis Kahn building.

←

Full-height glazing and wooden floors in the corridor soften the relatively strict lines of the architecture, allowing in light and views of the green surroundings.

Piano's logic, as always, is clear and light-filled. A combination of wooden floors
with some wood furnishings and otherwise light-colored surfaces provides sufficient
warmth while maintaining an image of efficiency.

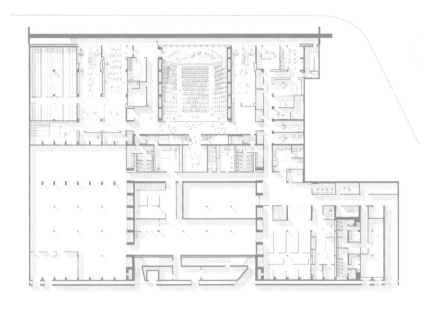

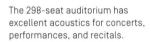

↑
A plan of Level B1 in the
Kimbell Museum extension
by Renzo Piano.

↓
The 298-seat auditorium has
excellent acoustics for concerts,
performances, and recitals.

LES TURBULENCES, FRAC CENTRE

2010–13

LOCATION 88 Rue du Vieux Colombier, 45000 Orléans, France,
+33 2 38 62 52 00, www.frac-centre.fr — AREA 3400 m² — CLIENT Région Centre
COST €8.5 million — COLLABORATION Electronic Shadow (Artists)

In describing Les Turbulences, Center for Contemporary Art and Architecture, the architects say that "the architectural idea was to take the entire site, which determines the surface of intervention, on which we identified two predominate grids emanating from the historic context of the site. The meeting and the convergence of these two geometries materialize in a deformation, a zone of turbulence, the future presence of the FRAC Centre." The extrusions resulting from the computer-designed overlapping of the grids house elements of the program: a temporary exhibition gallery in the tallest, an audiovisual gallery in the smallest, with a lobby, sales area, and a social space extending into the courtyard in the third. Interior and exterior cladding is in fine metallic and textile meshes capable of conveying a flow of information, which is transcribed in light images created by the collaboration with Electronic Shadow.

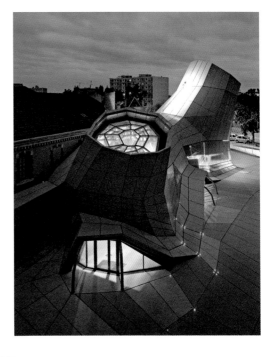

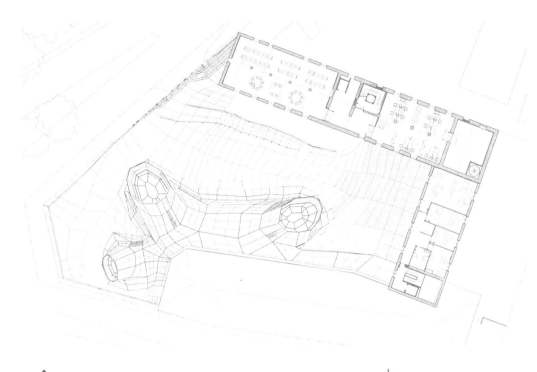

↑

A third floor plan of the complex shows the enveloping older structure and the insertion of the new building seen at the lower center of the drawing.

↓

Section drawings show the inside of the pavilion vis-à-vis the older structure.

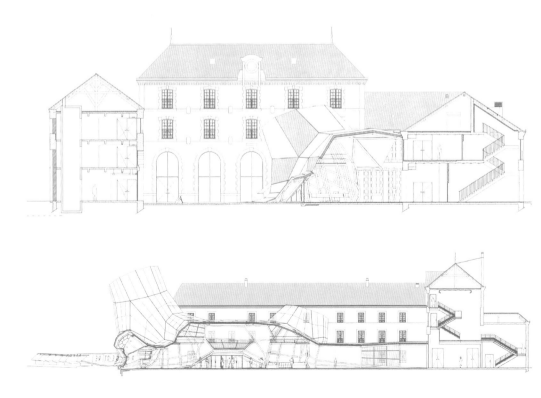

The unusual angular forms of the structure are as usual for Jakob + MacFarlane, and are based on computer models. More like a symbiotic creature than an incongruous contemporary element in the composition, Les Turbulences is sculptural in its form.

Frank O. Gehry

LOUIS VUITTON FOUNDATION

2008–14

LOCATION 8 Avenue du Mahatma Gandhi, Bois de Boulogne,
75116 Paris, France, +33 1 40 69 96 00, www.fondationlouisvuitton.fr — **AREA** 11 000 m²
CLIENT Fondation Louis Vuitton, Bernard Arnault, President

Commissioned by billionaire Bernard Arnault, head of the LVMH luxury goods group, the Louis Vuitton Foundation can, in many respects, be called Frank Gehry's masterpiece. In terms of inspiration and quality of construction, as well as its practicality for the exhibition of art, the Louis Vuitton Foundation goes beyond earlier works by the California architect. Located at the edge of the Jardin d'Acclimatation in Paris with views of the modern skyscrapers of La Défense, the building has highly visible elements made of wood and 13 500 square meters of glass, resembling "a glass cloud," according to the publicists, but also a ship with billowing sails. Gehry sought inspiration from the glass roofs of the Grand Palais and also from such structures as the nearby Palmarium (1893) in the Jardin des Serre d'Auteuil. One unusual aspect of the structure is that its base sits below grade, with a black granite cascade on one side and a surrounding reflecting pool. The decision to excavate the site was made in order to respect the height imposed by the Paris building code. Intended for the exhibition of modern and contemporary art, the Foundation includes 11 art galleries and an auditorium with capacity for 350 people, and the core of the building, dubbed the "Iceberg," is made of 19 000 separately molded sheets of fiber-reinforced Ductal concrete. The facility opened with such major works as a kaleidoscopic mirror and mosaic colonnade by Olafur Eliasson and a large gallery devoted to Gehry's own models for the building. As his models make clear, Gehry started not with the external forms, but with a series of boxes that represent the galleries, none of which are presented in the classic "enfilade" but which are scattered throughout the building and separated by neutral spaces. A visit to the Foundation cannot be complete without a tour of its numerous rooftop terraces that look down on the architecture and out toward the city.

↑
As seen from the street side, the building appears like a great glass ship, leaning into the wind.

↓
A waterfall and pond pass beneath the forward part of the building.

↑
Again from the street side, showing
the main entrance with the large Louis
Vuitton logo (LV).

↓
An east terrace plan shows the upper
part of the building, which is open to the
public at many points.

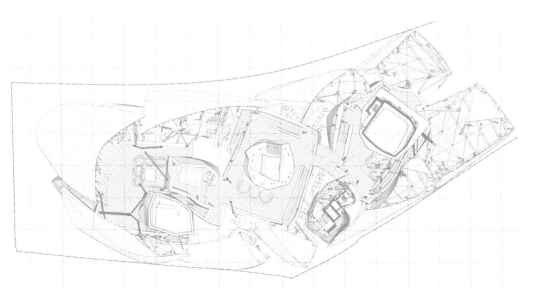

At night, the structure glows from within and hardly shows its means of support, almost floating above the ground like the fish sculptures by Frank Gehry seen in the café. Below, a fish-like form appears in the night.

Public access to the upper level terraces allows visitors to see the neighboring areas of the Bois de Boulogne, but also, in the distance (above), the Défense area of Paris.

Interior views show the extensive use of wooden beams beneath the outer glass shell of the building.

A ground level space near the café with the floating fish sculpture by the architect.

One of the shows for the inauguration of the
building was this presentation of Frank Gehry's
conceptual models for the Louis Vuitton Foundation, presented in a generously proportioned,
but darkened gallery.

Exhibition galleries provide for natural light where necessary and also for the high ceiling clearances needed for much contemporary art.

Anish Kapoor and Arata Isozaki

LUCERNE FESTIVAL ARK NOVA

2013

LOCATION Saigyo Modoshino-Matsu Koen, 23 Inuta, Matsushima-Aza, Matsushima, Miyagi, Japan, www.ark-nova.com/ www.lucernefestival.ch
AREA 720 m² — **CLIENT** ARK NOVA Executive Comultttee

Matsushima is located close to the areas most damaged by the 2011 Tohoku earthquake and tsunami, and the inflatable concert hall with capacity for 500 people—marking the first collaboration between Anish Kapoor and Arata Isozaki—was intended to reach out to as many people affected by those events as possible. Anish Kapoor developed the concept of the structure-less shell in collaboration with the British company Aerotrope, with whom he has worked on previous projects, and the form of the structure relates to his *Leviathan* (2011). PVC-coated polyester fiber fabric was used to make the interior and exterior structure, while floors were in salvaged cedar timber, and a used 12.2-meter freight container was employed as an air lock. A freely positioned, hanging, helium-filled, acoustic reflection balloon was used to ensure optimal sound inside the 18-meter-high hall.

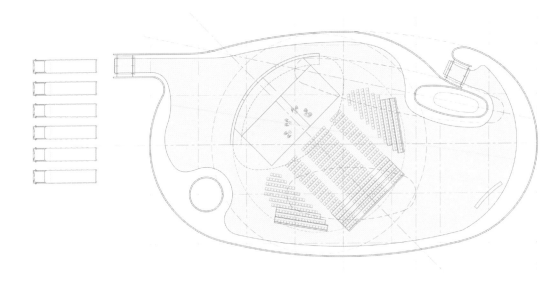

↑
A plan reveals the free form and how it can be used for seating.

↓
Photos show the assembly of the inflatable structure.

→

During the assembly process, a
view from within and up to the opening
in the skin of the structure.

↓

A view of the internal space fully in
place and lit.

MAR, ART MUSEUM OF RIO

2010-13

LOCATION Praça Mauá 5, Rio de Janeiro, RJ 20081–240, Brazil, +55 21 3031 2741, www.museudeartedorio.org.br — AREA 11 240 m² — CLIENT Prefeitura do Rio de Janeiro and Fundação RM — COLLABORATION Eza Viegas (Interior Design), Ricardo C. Branco (Coordinator), Veridiana Ruzzante (Team)

Three existing buildings with different architectural characteristics were unified to house the new Art Museum of Rio, the "A Escola do Olhar" school, as well as cultural and leisure spaces. The buildings concerned were the Palacete Dom João, a police building, and the old central bus station of Rio, and the museum project was considered part of the urban redevelopment of the historic downtown area of Rio. The architects created a "suspended square" on the roof of the police building with an "abstract and fluid form," uniting access and space for a bar and cultural events. Because of its ceiling heights and existing floor plan, the Palace was used for exhibition areas, and the police building for the school auditoriums, multimedia exhibition areas, administration, and employee areas of the complex.

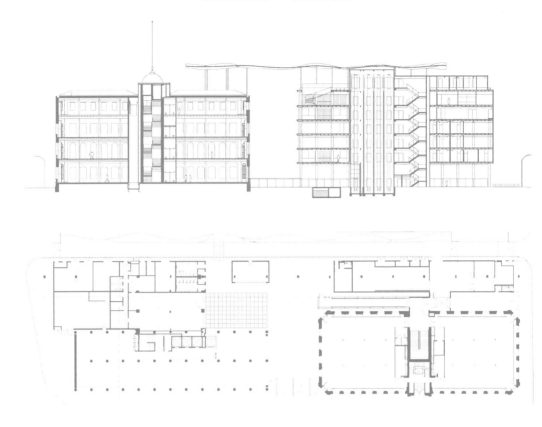

↑
A section drawing and a floor plan of the complex show its two, or actually three divided parts.

→
Planar surfaces mark the areas around the new building and cover the transition between the two structures, as seen in the section drawing above.

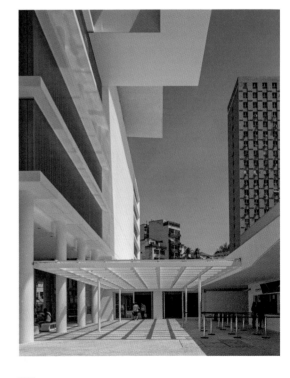

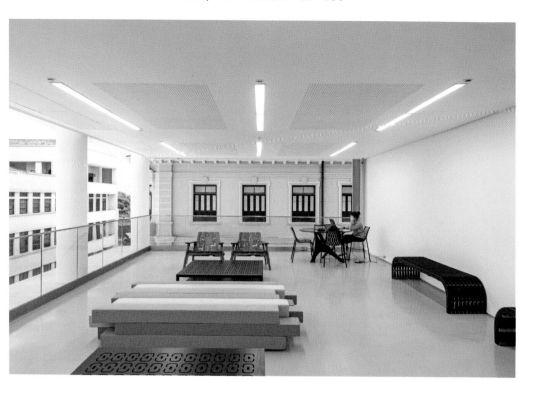

Interior spaces are bright and include such architectural features as this covered terrace (above) or the spectacular wood and metal spiral staircase below.

MARITIME MUSEUM OF DENMARK

2007–13

LOCATION Ny Kronborgvej 1, 3000 Helsingør, Denmark, +45 49 21 06 85, www.mfs.dk
AREA 7200 m² (including dock) — **CLIENT** Maritime Museum of Denmark / Museet for Søfart, Helsingør Municipality / Helsingør Kommune, A.P. Møller Foundation, JL Foundation — **COST** €44.4 million

This project involved the use of 466 anchors that were inserted 40 meters into the chalk bedrock of the site, creating—in the words of the architects—"a subterranean museum in a dry dock." They left the 60-year-old dock walls untouched, placing the galleries below ground and arranging them in a continuous loop around the dry dock walls. Thus the old dock is the focal point of the space, and creates an open, outdoor area where visitors can experience the scale of ship building. A series of three, double-level bridges span the exposed dry dock. The harbor bridge closes off the dock while serving as a harbor promenade; the museum's auditorium serves as a bridge connecting the adjacent Culture Yard with Kronborg Castle; and a sloping zigzag bridge brings visitors to the main entrance. This link unites the old and the new as visitors descend into the museum space overlooking the surroundings above and below ground. All floors, connecting exhibition spaces with the auditorium, classroom, offices, café, and the dock floor within the museum, slope gently. The history of the Maritime Museum of Denmark unfolds in a continuous sequence within and around the dock, seven meters below ground.

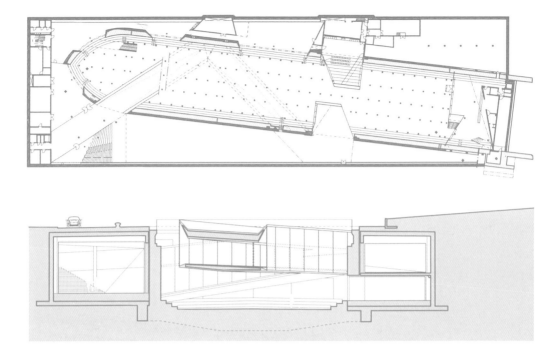

As plan, section, and the photo below show, the museum is placed in the existing dry dock rather like a ship, with visitors able to descend into the depths between the old walls, visible in the image of the café on the right.

The architects juxtapose concrete, wood and broadly glazed surfaces at the same time, creating a palette of muted colors.

←

Bjarne Ingels and his group adapted the principle of sloping spaces or passageways to the auditorium, which shares this feature.

MUSEO JUMEX

2012–13

LOCATION Miguel de Cervantes Saavedra 303,
Colonia Ampliación Granada, 11529 Mexico City, Mexico, +52 55 5395 2615/8,
www.fundacionjumex.org — AREA 6375 m² — CLIENT Eugenio López
COLLABORATION TAAU/Oscar Rodríguez

The architects describe the Museo Jumex "as a freestanding pavilion that corresponds to the eclectic nature of the neighboring buildings, which include the Museo Soumaya (Fernando Romero) and the underground Teatro Cervantes (Antón García-Abril)." Located in the Polanco area of Mexico City, the museum exhibits one of the largest private collections of contemporary art in Latin America. The design corresponds to the constraints imposed by the program and local planning rules, including the maximum allowed footprint. Given that the client's foundation has maintained its administration, storage facilities, library, and exhibition areas at existing premises in Ecatepec, the new building is intended in good part for temporary shows and exhibition of the Jumex collection. The primary exhibition space is on the upper floors, where natural overhead light is available. "Consisting of a steel structure with west-facing roof lights and a horizontal diffuser layer, the roof distributes light evenly to illuminate the artworks and create an ambient light for the space," say the architects. The plinth, 14 columns, ground- and first-floor cores, and the soffits are made of exposed white concrete, while the façades, the roof, and the floors from the plinth upwards are clad in travertine marble from Xalapa, Veracruz. Full-height glazing is set in stainless-steel frames.

←
The relatively opaque surface of the
building does not necessarily indicate its
precise function or the degree of natural
light that is admitted by the design.

A section drawing on the right and the
photo on the left page shows the successive angled roofs that are positioned to
bring natural light into the museum.

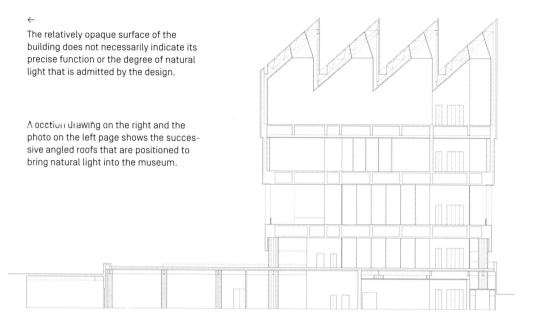

↓
With an elegance that is typical of David Chipperfield, a large
pivoting door or wall surface allows ingress, contrasting with full-
height glazing held in thin, refined stainless steel frames.

Natural daylight is suffused into the upper level gallery spaces. Black surfaces contrast with lighter ones where angles and views through the spaces, such as the stairway to the left, animate the visit.

Massimiliano and Doriana Fuksas

NEW NATIONAL ARCHIVES OF FRANCE

2009-13

LOCATION 59 Rue Guynemer, 93383 Pierrefitte-sur-Seine, Saint-Denis, France, +33 1 75 47 20 00, www.archivesnationales.culture.gouv.fr/pierrefitte/contact.html — **AREA** 108 136 m²
CLIENT French Ministry of Culture and Communication — **COLLABORATION** Antony Gormley

The genesis of the project is explained by the architects in these words: "The initial choice was to investigate the site and its characteristics in both territorial and sociocultural contexts to reveal a unique identity." The New National Archives of France is composed of two main "bodies": one that extends horizontally, "suspended, lightweight, transparent"; the other with a tension in height, "anchored to the ground, imposing, reflective." Cantilevered volumes in the horizontal block, with large glazed volumes, contain offices, a conference room, and an exhibition room. The actual archives are in the monolithic anchored volume with aluminum cladding or "skin" with a lozenge geometry that is also seen in the glass façades of the "satellite" volumes. A double-height hall is located at the main entrance, where a work by the artist Susanna Fritscher marks the space, while the red "Carla" chair chosen for the conference room was designed by the architect and manufactured by Poltrona Frau. Outside, basins surmounted by walkways surround parts of the complex, which is enriched by contemporary sculpture: one by Antony Gormley is sited between the monolithic archives and the satellite volumes, in front of which stands another, a series of concrete "strongboxes" by Pascal Convert.

A plan and elevation show the complexity and density of the structure. Here, as in his Shenzhen Airport Terminal (see p. 150), the architect takes on the complexities of a very large official facility and renders the space varied and convivial.

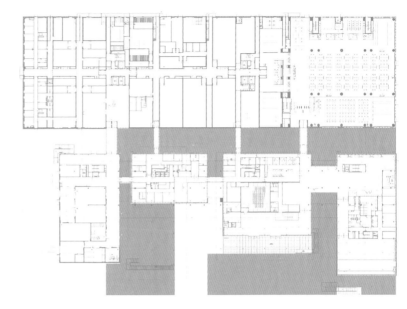

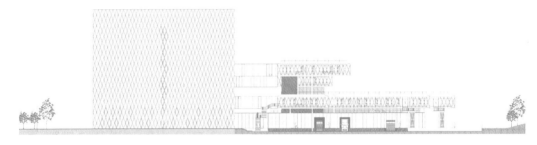

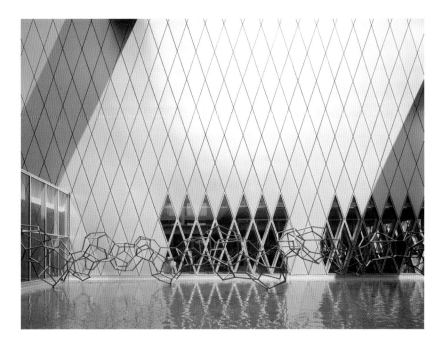

Using diamond-shaped panels and providing for ample natural light, as in the generous space below, Fuksas brings what could have been a dull building to life.

PÉREZ ART MUSEUM MIAMI (PAMM)

2010-13

LOCATION 1103 Biscayne Boulevard, Miami, FL 33132, USA, +1 305 375 3000, www.pamm.org
GROSS FLOOR AREA 11 125 m² — **CLIENT** Miami Art Museum

Standing in Museum Park on Biscayne Bay and near the Frost Museum of Science, PAMM is lifted off the ground to make sure that it is well above storm surge levels. A canopy creates a "veranda-like public space that welcomes visitors to the museum and the park" and a broad stairway connects the museum platform facing the bay to a waterfront promenade. Generous glazing on the façade is recessed to reduce solar gain, while tropical plants intended to help in the creation of a microclimate "engulf the structural system." Contrasting with the familiar "white box" type of gallery, the art spaces inside employ concrete and wood in different combi-

With its large flat roof and thin columns, the PAMM has a distinctive profile generated by the suspended white-box forms and hanging vegetation.

nations, "reflecting the outside materials of the building." Four different gallery types—called Overview, Focus, Project, and Special Exhibition galleries—form the space for art on part of the first and the entire second floor, all with large openings with views to the park, city, and bay, and with a stairway broad enough to double as an auditorium connecting the two exhibition levels. The museum shop and bistro are on the platform level, oriented to the bay, with open-air parking located below the building, while education and research facilities are on the third floor, along with museum offices.

The museum sits on the water's edge and contrasts with
the high-rise buildings seen behind it (above). Parking is on
the lower level and the museum spaces are lifted off the
ground to protect it from potential storm water levels.

As always, Herzog & de Meuron succeed in creating an unexpected
architectural solution to the particular situation of this museum.
The unusual hanging vegetation and high veranda-like area facing
the water accentuate the presence of the building.

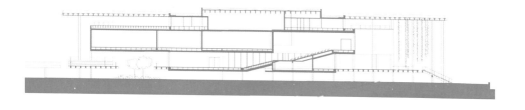

Images of the exhibition galleries with natural light controlled as necessary and ample height for works of contemporary art.

↑
A drawing of Level 2 and a section drawing.

SERPENTINE GALLERY SUMMER PAVILION 2013

2013

LOCATION Kensington Gardens, London, UK — **AREA** 357 m² — **CLIENT** Serpentine Gallery
COLLABORATION Nadine de Ripainsel, Keisuke Kiri, Ryo Tsuchie

Sou Fujimoto is the third Japanese architect to design a temporary Serpentine Gallery Summer Pavilion, following Toyo Ito (2002) and SANAA (2009), and the youngest architect ever to receive this commission. Made of 20-millimeter white steel poles erected in a latticework pattern, the pavilion did not resemble any known form of building, a fact that is in keeping with the architect's intense search for new types of architecture. Intended to be a flexible, multipurpose space, the structure contained a café, but above all encouraged visitors to reflect on the relation of this structure to the natural environment and surely also to the more formal design of the neighboring Serpentine Gallery itself. Fujimoto states: "It is a really fundamental question how architecture is different from nature, or how architecture can be part of nature, or how they can be merged . . . what are the boundaries between nature and artificial things?"

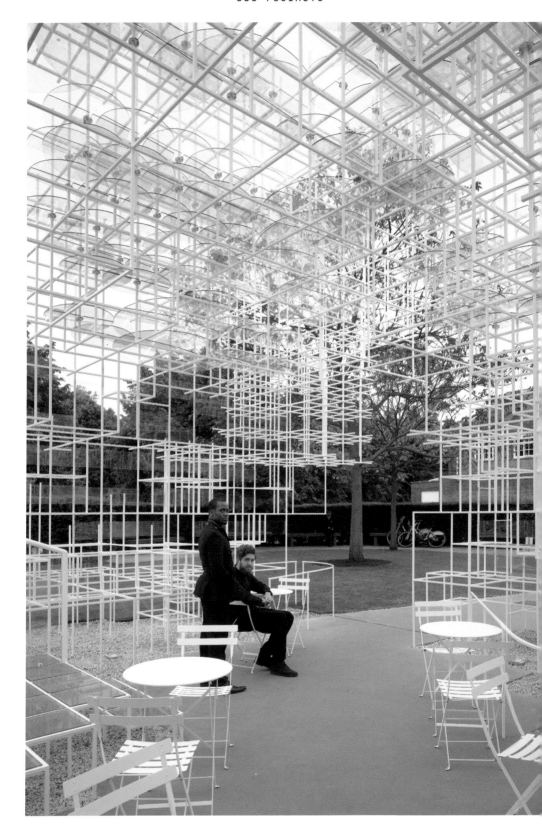

Sou Fujimoto has long endeavored to challenge the very bases of architecture, and in this instance, although there is no doubt that he has created a pavilion, there are neither walls nor ceilings in the usual sense of the terms.

→

A site plan shows that the structure itself is permeable from nearly all directions, allowing views of the park but also gatherings.

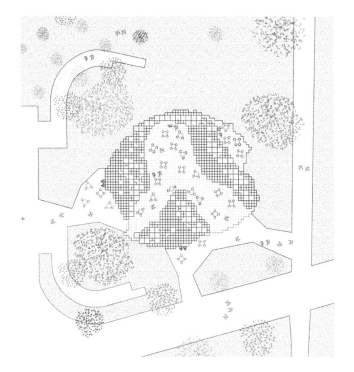

SIEGERLAND HIGHWAY CHURCH

2011–13

LOCATION Autohof Wilnsdorf (Exit 23), Elkersberg, 57234 Wilnsdorf, Germany, www.autobahnkirche-siegerland.de **AREA** 240 m²
CLIENT Autobahnkirchenverein Siegerland e.V. — **COST** €1.5 million
COLLABORATION Holzbau Amann GmbH, Elacoat GmbH, Schreinerei Hein GmbH

Starting with a two-dimensional plan, the architects developed a three-dimensional structure using parametric design techniques with Rhino and Grasshopper software. Schneider+schumacher Parametrik helped to design a finely detailed wooden ribbed structure that optimized both the material and the construction down to the last detail. The timber inner dome sitting on the basically square plan of the Siegerland Highway Church offers natural lighting. Interior furnishings were developed in close collaboration with the client and, like the inner dome, are made of wood. The architects state that the "presbytery, podium, altar, and the backlit cross are painted in a pure white to reflect sunlight, and therewith seem dematerialized." The structure is made essentially of wood, concrete, and polyurethane boards.

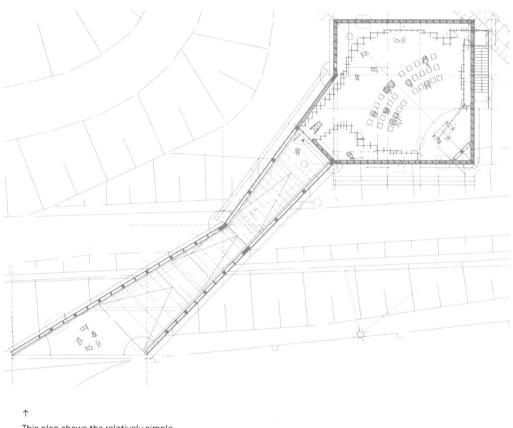

↑
This plan shows the relatively simple,
if unusual configuration of the chapel
with its long approach walls and main,
nearly square space

→
The section drawing reveals the spire
and also the arcing wooden shell that
forms the space around the altar, seen
on the lower part of the right page.

Though its placement next to signs for Total and
Burger King might be found surprising, the white presence
of the chapel attracts attention and surely curiosity.

ST. LOUIS ART MUSEUM

2009–13

LOCATION 1 Fine Arts Drive, Forest Park, St. Louis, MO 63110–1380, USA,
+1 314 721 0072, www.slam.org —**AREA** 9000 m² — **CLIENT** St. Louis Art Museum
COLLABORATION HOK (Architect of Record)

Cass Gilbert designed the original, main building of the St. Louis Art Museum as one of the exhibition pavilions for the 1904 St. Louis World's Fair, which became the City Art Museum in 1909. Extensions and renovations were carried out in the 1950s, 1980, and 1985, and David Chipperfield's new single-story East Pavilion seeks to keep "its visual impact on the immediate surroundings and its wider environment to a minimum." The building is erected on a low plinth so that the floor level maintains that of the main floor of the older Gilbert building. Used for the modern and

Next to its stony 1904 neighbor, the Chipperfield building projects a calm classicism that is clearly very contemporary in its choice of materials and design. There is no conflict with the older structure, only an elegant and appropriate complementarity.

SAINT LOUIS ART MUSEUM

contemporary art collection of the museum, the East Pavilion also provides temporary exhibition spaces, a museum shop, a large dining space, and 300 parking spaces. Landscaping around the building offers a forecourt, as well as sculpture gardens that are blended into the city's surrounding Forest Park. Dark concrete paneled façades were cast and polished on site, while a coffered concrete ceiling allows modulated natural light into the building.

The architect succeeds in creating forms that are at once powerful and understated. Contemporary art, as seen in the image below or on the right page, is very much at home in the gallery spaces.

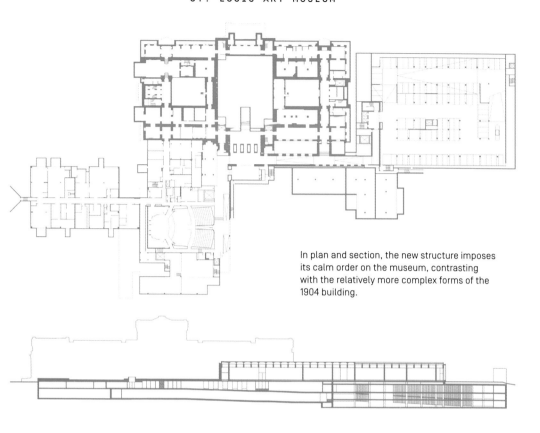

In plan and section, the new structure imposes its calm order on the museum, contrasting with the relatively more complex forms of the 1904 building.

↓
The architect affirms a ceiling grid that allows the art to be clearly visible, bathed in natural and/or artificial light.

317

John Pawson

ST. MORITZ CHURCH INTERIOR REMODELING

2011–13

LOCATION Moritzplatz 5, 86150 Augsburg, Germany, +49 82 12 59 25 30, www.moritzkirche.de
AREA 1857 m² — CLIENT Diocese of St. Moritz — COST €3.7 million
COLLABORATION Jan Hobel (Project Architect)

The St. Moritz Church was founded nearly 1000 years ago. According to the architects, "the purpose of this latest intervention has been to retune the existing architecture, from aesthetic, functional, and liturgical perspectives, with considerations of sacred atmosphere always at the heart of the project." Elements of the façade and selected artifacts were "pared away" or relocated in order to "clear the visual field." An existing architectural focus on the apse was reinforced, while glass in the apse windows was replaced with thin pieces of onyx. This gesture created a luminous wrapping for a Baroque sculpture, the *Christus Salvator* by Georg Petel. Baroque clerestory windows serve as other sources of indirect light, whereas a further alteration involved the relocation of the altar to a new island in the nave, closer to the congregation in accordance with the requirements of the Second Vatican Council. The overall result is a kind of white simplicity that those who know John Pawson's work will find very familiar, despite the Baroque setting.

John Pawson is known as a master of minimalism. A point he
makes here and in other restoration work is that such minimalism
can be found even in older buildings.

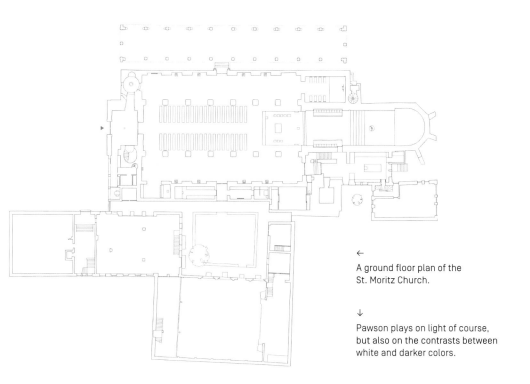

←
A ground floor plan of the
St. Moritz Church.

↓

Pawson plays on light of course,
but also on the contrasts between
white and darker colors.

Preston Scott Cohen

TAIYUAN MUSEUM OF ART

2009-13

LOCATION Taiyuan, China, latitude 37.88692855834961, longitude 112.54199981689453
AREA 32 500 m^2 — **CLIENT** Taiyuan City Government
COST $50 million — **COLLABORATION** Amit Nemlich (Project Architect),
Architecture Design Institute of South East University

Conceived as a cluster of buildings, the architects explain that the Taiyuan Museum of Art "responds to the urban parkscape in which it is set; visitors are encouraged to pass through the building while not entering into the museum itself." It includes an auditorium, bookstore, restaurant, library, education center, and administrative wing, while the exhibition galleries are intended for maximum flexibility allowing for the spaces to be organized into "a single, spiraling sequence for large chronological exhibitions or into autonomous clusters operating indepen-

dently." Visitors can either follow a predetermined sequence or wander from one gallery to another in a "non-linear fashion." In addition, again in the words of the architects: "Exterior lightweight honeycomb panels with stone veneer produce an evocative and elusive material effect and the perception of an exceptional scale. The panels are reflective as if metallic, seemingly too large to be stone panels, but clearly possessing the properties of both materials. Advanced parametric software allowed panels to conform to standard widths, reducing material waste."

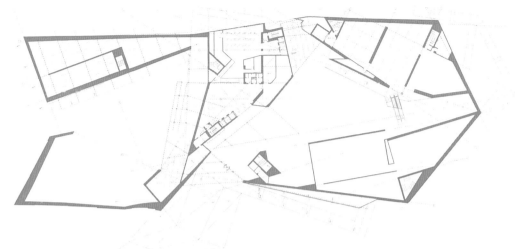

↑
A plan shows the internal disposition of the spaces.

Seen from the outside with its dramatic cantilevers and skewed forms, the museum certainly is the object of attention and attraction.

The dynamic exterior of the museum clearly implies an equally dynamic interior, where daylight enters frequently and grand atrium spaces, like the ones seen here, give an impression that all concerned have worked to create an exceptional piece of architecture.

THE ARC—RIVER CULTURE MULTIMEDIA THEATER PAVILION

2012

LOCATION 751 Jukgok-ri, Dasa-eup Dalseong-gun, Daegu, South Korea (257 m N)
AREA 3200 m² — **CLIENT** Kwater — **COLLABORATION** John Guida, Josh Dannenberg, Brian Deluna, Duho Choi, Hong Min Kim, Allison Austin

Built with a steel frame covered with silver fritted ETFE pillows, the visible part of the pavilion sits above a concealed exhibition gallery that contains "an immersive multimedia environment illuminated only by projections of the abstracted and re-conceptualized qualities of the surrounding site. The architecture," states Asymptote, "enables the visitor's experience to be an alternating play between a 'real' experience of the water, sky, and landscape that surrounds the building, and a virtual experience as presented through multimedia." On the roof, an observation deck and a reflecting pond allow visitors to see the actual natural landscape and water that surrounds the pavilion's location on a peninsula. A variety of brightly lit colors on the underside of the construction give the visible structure a constantly changing appearance.

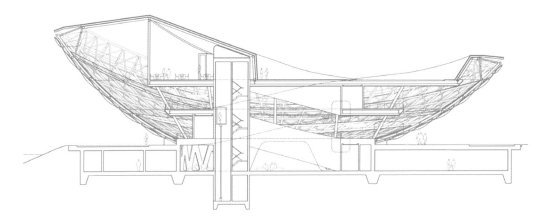

↑
A section drawing of the complex shows the theater.
The form of the building might be likened to a stylized crib.

↓
An aerial view shows the peninsula on which it was built.

Inside the theater, the curving lines
and saturated colors employed are
in harmony with the rather surprising
outside appearance of the structure.

Marco Casagrande

ULTRA RUIN

2013

LOCATION Yangming Mountain, Yangminghsan National Park, between Taipei City and New Taipei City, Taiwan — **AREA** 210 m² (interior), 520 m² (terrace) — **CLIENT** Aaron Lee **COLLABORATION** Nikita Wu, Frank Chen, Yu-Chen Chiu

Growing out from the ruins of an abandoned red-brick farmhouse set at the juncture of agricultural terraces and the jungle, this home's "weak architecture follows the principles of Open Form." According to Marco Casagrande, the design was "improvised on the site based on instincts reacting to the presence of jungle, ruin, and local knowledge." Used essentially by the family of the owners, the building is occasionally used for larger meetings, but has fully flexible space that is often defined as being between exterior and interior, rather than settling in a marked fashion for one or the other. Casagrande seeks to make place for "nature and human error" to rule the development of this project rather than any grand preconceived scheme. He states: "Ultra Ruin is more of an organic accident, than based on industrial control. Accident is greater than architectural control. Architectural control has been opened up in order to let nature step in and human error take place. In order to understand the dynamics of an accident, one must be present. To be present is the key of all art."

Passageways and spaces that are only
partially covered give an impression of an
almost organic architecture, intimately
related to its site, both built and natural.

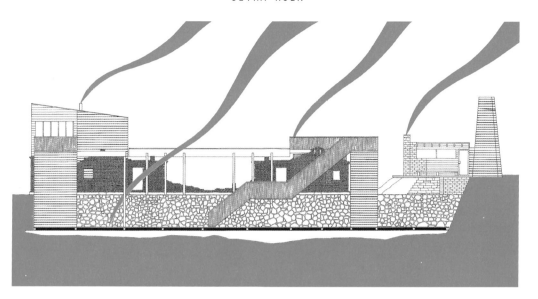

↑
The drawing shows the ruins of the old farm in dark green and the additions in grey.

↓
An outdoor covered space exemplifies what Marco Casagrande calls "weak" architecture, unimposing and functional.

Zaiga Gaile

ŽANIS LIPKE MEMORIAL

2008–12

LOCATION Mazais Balasta Dambis 8, Riga 1048, Latvia, www.lipke.lv — AREA 282 m²
CLIENT Žanis Lipke Memorial Association — COST €400 000 — CONCEPT Māris Gailis, Viktors Jansons, Augusts Sukuts — COLLABORATION Ingmār Atavs, Kristaps Ģelzis, Reinis Suhanovs

During the occupation of Latvia by Nazi Germany (1941–44), more than 60 000 Jews died in concentration camps. Among the most prominent Latvians who attempted to aid the Jews were Žanis and Johanna Lipke, a working-class couple who saved the lives of more than 50 people, helping them to escape the Riga Ghetto and concentration camps by hiding them in a bunker under a woodshed in their garden. In 1967 the Lipkes received the "Righteous Among the Nations" award from the Yad Vashem Memorial for their work. The architects describe the Žanis Lipke Memorial—which was built next to the Lipkes's family house—as an "ascetic windowless building made of dark gray wood resembling an overturned boat resting onshore, like a ferryman's boat that has completed its mission." An open shaft in the center of the building unites three levels and looks down into a concrete bunker of the original 3 × 3-meter dimensions.

→
A section drawing shows the architects' idea of an "overturned boat,"
while the plan below indicates a strict
rectangular form.

The dark wood interiors of the building,
admitting little natural light, evoke
the time of the concentration camps
without being unduly explicit. There is,
rather, a sense of foreboding or atone-
ment in this design.

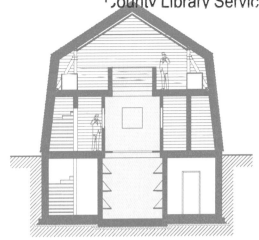

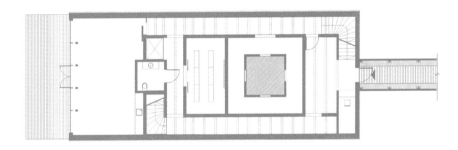

CULTURE & RELIGION

LE
ISU
RE

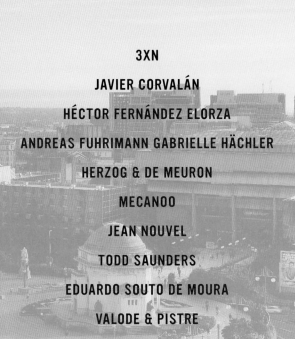

3XN

JAVIER CORVALÁN

HÉCTOR FERNÁNDEZ ELORZA

ANDREAS FUHRIMANN GABRIELLE HÄCHLER

HERZOG & DE MEURON

MECANOO

JEAN NOUVEL

TODD SAUNDERS

EDUARDO SOUTO DE MOURA

VALODE & PISTRE

Javier Corvalán

APG PUBLIC GOLF DRIVING RANGE

2013

LOCATION Av. Ñu Guazu, Luque, Paraguay — AREA 1500 m²
CLIENT Asociación Paraguaya de Golf

An 80-meter-long façade of the Driving Range structure splits the 32 500-square-meter site into two playing areas. Spaces for putting and chipping greens are opposite the south front of the building, while on the other (rear) side of the structure a 300-meter driving range has been installed. The building itself houses offices, a pro shop, lounge, bar, golf school, and bathrooms, all located on the ground level. The architect explains that the "construction is

Corvalán's sculptural structure is quite un-like any other building. With its zigzag form and cantilevered leading edge, it forms a useful division between two playing areas.

based on a low-maintenance concept, with fully visible concrete or rough stone walls deriving from the fact that the property is exposed to extreme weather conditions to which only heavy construction offers a practical response. The project proposes a timeless and neutral language where the structure itself is the form, function, and aesthetics."

The powerful concrete and stone form is
intended to resist difficult weather conditions
and to require little or no maintenance.

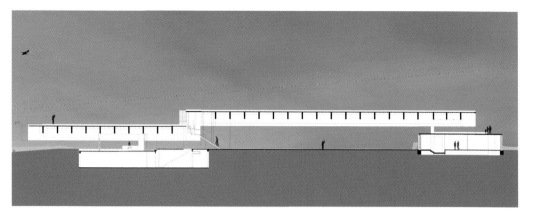

↑
A section drawing shows
the ground level pro shop
and other usable spaces.

→
The metal ladder has a light
structure that seems to contrast with the heavy concrete
and stone of the building.

BEIRUT SOUKS ENTERTAINMENT CENTER

2010–14

LOCATION Allenby Street, Beirut, Lebanon — **AREA** 20 000 m² — **CLIENT** Solidere
COLLABORATION Annabel Karim Kassar & Associes (Local Architect)

Located very close to Rafael Moneo's Beirut Souks, and built for the same client (Solidere), this project was an indirect result of the international competition organized for the Souks themselves, of which Valode & Pistre were co-winners (Moneo did not participate). It is also close to the restored Foch-Allenby area, the "French quarter" of downtown Beirut. The architects explain that the new Entertainment Center was "designed as an urban project playing a role in the spatial definition of the squares, placettes, and streets. Its sculptural morphology, made up of an assembly of metal ribbons forming a coppery arabesque in space, and its façades, animated with points of light that form changing images, make the building an emblem of the new, nocturnal life of Beirut."

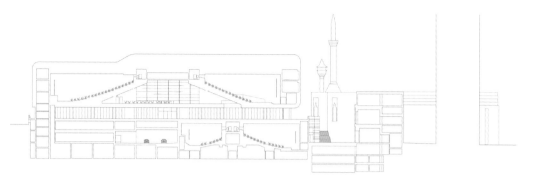

↑
A section drawing with the cinema
areas clearly visible. The minarets
to the right are part of a neighboring
mosque.

↓
The new building is located just opposite Rafael Moneo's Beirut Souks in an
area completely restored by Solidere.

Todd Saunders

FOGO ISLAND INN

2010–13

LOCATION Joe Batt's Arm, Fogo Island, NL A0G 2X0, Canada, +1 855 268 9277, www.fogoislandinn.ca —**AREA** 4500 m² — **CLIENT** Shorefast Foundation, Zita Cobb, Anthony Cobb **COLLABORATION** Sheppard Case Architects Inc. (Architect of Record)

Created at the request of the Shorefast Foundation, the Fogo Island Inn is intended to "be a cultural and economic engine for Fogo Island, one of Canada's oldest settlements; created in response to a pressing need to find new relevance for traditional knowledge and traditional ways." The X-shaped structure has a two-story, east-west volume with public spaces and a four-story, southwest-to-northeast section running parallel to the coast, containing 29 guest rooms. Public areas include an art gallery curated by Fogo Island Arts; a dining room, bar, and lounge which was recently rated as one of the top 10 new restaurants in Canada; and a heritage library for the collection of the late Dr. Leslie Harris, former president of Memorial University of Newfoundland. The second floor includes a cinema, while the fourth-floor roof deck has saunas and outdoor hot tubs with views of the sea. Ecological concerns are taken into account throughout the project, as the architect's words illutrate: "Traditional-style 'shore' legs are used to support the floors while minimizing the overall building footprint and the impact on the adjacent rocks, lichens, and berries."

←
Interior spaces offer plunging views to the shoreline.

↓
A room with an unimpeded ocean view.

↑
A seaside hot tub allows clients
to enjoy the view in comfort.

↓
The double-height dining space with
an almost completely glazed corner.

LIBRARY OF BIRMINGHAM WITH THE REP THEATER

2010–13

LOCATION Centenary Square, Broad Street, Birmingham B1 2ND, UK, +44 121 242 42 42, www.libraryofbirmingham.com / Broad Street, Birmingham B1 2EP, UK, +44 12 12 36 44 55, www.birmingham-rep.co.uk — **AREA** 35 000 m² — **CLIENT** Birmingham City Council — **COST** £186 million

The Library of Birmingham includes adult and children's libraries, study spaces, a music library, a business and learning center, multimedia facilities, archives, the Shakespeare Memorial Room, roof gardens and terraces, offices, a climate-controlled gallery, cafés, and a lounge area. The project also included a new 300-seat auditorium shared with the neighboring Repertory Theater (REP) and the urban plan for Centenary Square, the largest public square in the city. The Library of Birmingham is a transparent glass building with a concrete frame and lift cores, and an aluminum façade. Interiors are clad in slate, oak, and ceramic tiles for the flooring, with open-cell metal ceilings. It is organized around eight internal circular spaces, while the Shakespeare Memorial Room, designed in 1882, is located in a rooftop rotunda. Careful attention was paid to energy use, earning the structure a BREEAM excellence rating.

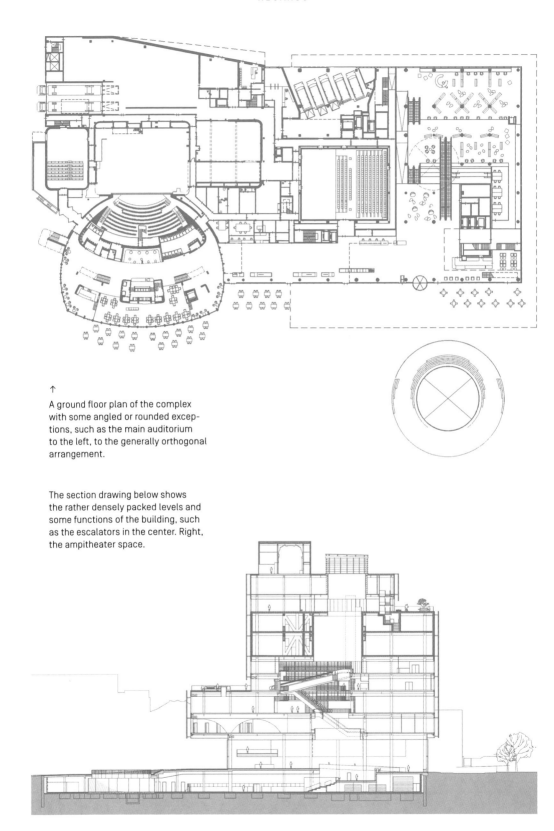

↑
A ground floor plan of the complex with some angled or rounded exceptions, such as the main auditorium to the left, to the generally orthogonal arrangement.

The section drawing below shows the rather densely packed levels and some functions of the building, such as the escalators in the center. Right, the ampitheater space.

↑
The studio theater seating about 300 people is part of the library facilities but is shared with the neighboring Rep.

→
The reconstituted 1882 Shakespeare Memorial Room from the Birmingham Central Library.

←
The Rotunda. The architects have orchestrated a series of interconnecting levels alternating with open spaces that at once give an impression of density and a certain freedom.

↑
Bookshelf space and seating in the Rotunda for young people.

←
The foyer area of the Rep Theater (top) and stack spaces with reading areas (below).

→
A curved and fully glazed façade looks out to the amphitheater space that can be used for outdoor performances.

MULTIPURPOSE PAVILION

2009–13

LOCATION Viana do Castelo, Portugal
AREA 5942 m² — CLIENT Municipality of Viana do Castelo — COST €12 million
COLLABORATION Diogo Guimarães, Ricardo Rosa Santos, João Queiróz

Eduardo Souto de Moura's Multipurpose Pavilion, described as an "aluminum box," is located near buildings by Fernando Távora (Praça da Liberdade) and Álvaro Siza (Public Library, 2001–07). It is related by the architect to naval architecture and in particular to the museum-ship called the "Gil Eanes," which is docked in Viana do Castelo. Intended for cultural and sporting events, the steel and reinforced-concrete structure can be entered from the north or south sides. The architect describes the interior as "ample and permeable, offering the possibility of viewing the sea from the entrance floor." The ground-floor façades are in glass with aluminum frames; the pillars are in plaster; and the roof is in aluminum.

Eduardo Souto de Moura gives a relatively hard, almost industrial appearance to much of this building and yet alternates this effect with surprising openings.

↓

The central area used for sports can also accommodate extra seating for events.

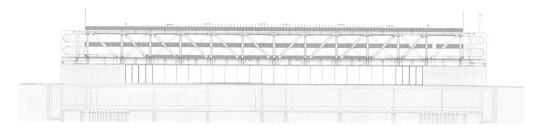

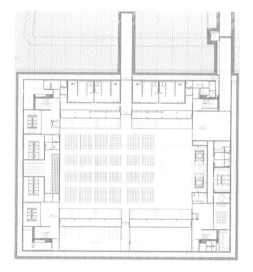

Above, an elevation drawing and left, a plan of level 1.

↓

The shower area is minimal to say the least, fitting in with the hard-edge feeling of most of the building.

Jean Nouvel

RENAISSANCE BARCELONA FIRA HOTEL

2008-12

LOCATION Plaza Europa 50–52, L'Hospitalet de Llobregat, 08902 Barcelona, Spain, +34 932 61 80 00,
www.marriott.com/hotels/travel/bcnrf-renaissance-barcelona-fira-hotel — AREA 22 000 m²
CLIENT Hoteles Catalonia — COLLABORATION Ribas & Ribas Arquitectos

Full-height outside loggias unite the
110-meter-high double tower of the 358-bed-
room Renaissance Barcelona Fira Hotel
in the Hospitalet de Llobregat area in the
south of Barcelona in a sort of "vertical
landscape" of palm trees, planted on every
level and crowning the top of the building
where the suite terraces, the fitness area,
and swimming pool are located. Rather than
visible windows, the white east-, south-, and
west-facing façades and the black north-
facing façade show a repetitive pattern that
filters and enhances natural light, at the
same time as it makes the appearance of
the building change according to the time of
day. Indeed, as the architects remark: "The
lighting effects are unstable. They slip into
the bedrooms. On walls, ceilings, curtains,
sheets. ..." This project was carried out by
Ateliers Jean Nouvel in close collaboration
with Ribas & Ribas Architects, a local firm
founded in 1957.

← The architects evoke "a luxuriant vertical landscape, lined with the passageways of bedrooms and crossed by a 'Piranesian' game constituted by the terraces and the staircases."

↓ There are "no windows but openings that take shape and merge in plant printed patterns on glass and 'esgrafiados' in concrete."

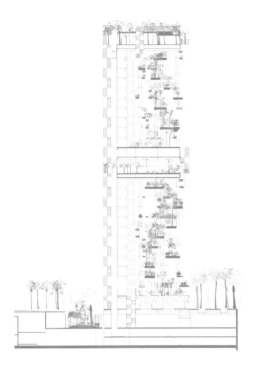

↑
A section drawing renders explicit the spiraling presence of greenery in the hotel, also seen in the image above right.

↓
A more minimally designed bar space.

Andreas Fuhrimann Gabrielle Hächler

ROTSEE FINISH TOWER

2012-13

LOCATION Lucerne, Switzerland, www.naturarena.ch — **AREA** 177 m² — **CLIENT** Naturarena Rotsee — **COST** €1 million — **COLLABORATION** Carlo Fumarola, Daniel Stankowski

Set on a lake that is popular with rowers, this three-story viewing tower is part of the first phase of the Naturarena Rotsee area development, with a Rowing Center scheduled to open in July 2016. The Finish Tower and the future Rowing Center are meant to form a single architectural ensemble. The prefabricated pine wood design sits on a pillared concrete platform set just above water level. The wood is treated with an innovative method that reduces water absorption, increasing its durability considerably. The architects wished to create a hybrid structure—"a functional active building on one side, and a sculpture in the lake on the other." Used only about three weeks per year in the summer, the tower generally remains closed the rest of the year. Inside, there are three levels; one for the International Rowing Federation (FISA), one for Jury and Timing, and a space for an Event Speaker.

←
The Finish Tower with its folding shutters in the open position.

↓
A light staircase offers access to the second level above the water.

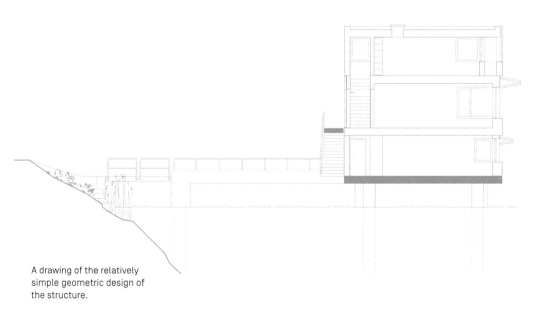

A drawing of the relatively simple geometric design of the structure.

↓

Interior finishings are nearly as minimal as the building itself.

THE BLUE PLANET

2010–13

LOCATION Jacob Fortlingsvej 1, 2770 Kastrup, Denmark, +45 44 22 22 44, www.denblaaplanet.dk
GROSS AREA 10 000 m² — **CLIENT** Bygningsfonden 'Den Blå Planet' — **COST** €97.3 million
COLLABORATION Stig Vesterager Gothelf, Ida S. Greisen, Torsten Wang

The Blue Planet is Denmark's new national aquarium, focusing on all types of aquatic life—from cold and warm areas, and fresh and salt water. Located on an elevated site opposite the sea north of the harbor of Kastrup, the almost entirely white structure resembles the shape of a starfish when seen from planes approaching the nearby airport of Copenhagen. The architects explain that the form of the building was inspired by a "great whirlpool," while the façade, made up of 33 000 diamond-shaped aluminum shingles, "is reminiscent of fish scales." The project includes 5000 square meters of exhibition space, with an outdoor area—with ponds announcing the aquatic theme of the interior—that covers a further 2000 square meters. Inside, the entrance sequence is located in the longest of the "arms" of the whirlpool pattern while a circular foyer invites visitors to explore rivers, lakes, and the ocean. A mixture of light, sound, advanced audiovisual technology, projections, film, interactivity, graphics, illustrations, and signs aimed at all age levels are integrated into the museum presentation. In total, the Blue Planet contains about seven million liters of water and 53 aquariums and displays.

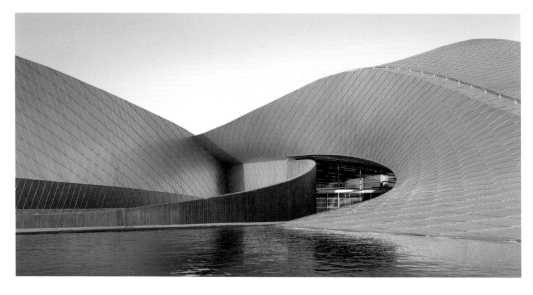

↑
Visitors enter through a passage flanked by a pond, almost giving the impression that they are wading into the building.

The curving exterior forms are not specifically organic but they do evoke a relation to nature.

The darkened inside of parts of
the interior gives way to some of
the 53 aquariums and displays.

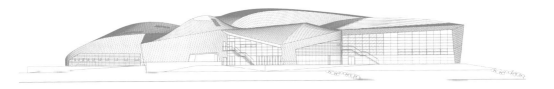

→

The "whirlpool" design is most clearly evident in the plan to the right.

↓

A circular foyer is the central point of navigation within the Blue Planet. Here visitors can choose which river, lake, or ocean to explore.

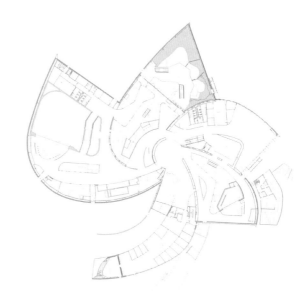

Héctor Fernández Elorza

VENECIA PARK

2009–12

LOCATION Glorieta de la Calle Zafiro, s/n, 50007 Zaragoza, Spain, www.parquevenecia.com
AREA 12 ha — **CLIENT** Junta de Compensación 88-1 — **COST** €4.1 million
COLLABORATION Manuel Fernández (Architect)

The architect was required to specifically address three issues in the project for Venecia Park: "The resolution of an acoustic problem, the evacuation of rainfall, and the question of topography." Noise results from traffic on the Ronda Hispanidad (Third Ring Road) so a wall acting as a sound barrier—100 meters long with a maximum height of 10 meters—was erected on the flatter southwest side of the park to block this. A 3150-square-meter basin was designed to deal with heavy rainfall, and serves as a pedestrian square most of the year. A difference in ground level of no less than 14 meters between the Ring Road and a new residential area was solved with reinforced-earth walls, galvanized-steel mesh, and large stones. Interconnected, staggered platforms with small squares and light metal pergolas, pine trees, and pedestrian ramps make up the rest of the design.

← A large wall made with reinforced earth, steel mesh, and large stones marks one edge of the project.

↓ A cross-section drawing of the design.

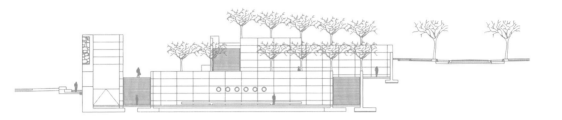

↓ The required pubic square was created bordered by powerful walls that mask the substantial 14-meter difference in ground level from one end of the site to the other.

VOLKSHAUS BASEL, BAR, BRASSERIE

2011–12

LOCATION Rebgasse 12–14, 4058 Basel, Switzerland, +41 61 690 93 10, www.volkshaus-basel.ch/en
AREA 5447 m² — **CLIENT** Volkshaus Basel Immobilien AG

Originally a medieval manor—the Burgvogtei—stood on this site, which is close to Basel's Messe fairground. In 1845, a brewery with a restaurant was built here, which expanded in 1874 to house a beer and a concert hall. When the premises were taken over by the city of Basel in 1905, the facilities became a hub of political, social, and cultural activities. The new Volks-haus Basel was built in 1925, incorporating the existing concert hall and expanded to include halls of various sizes, offices, conference rooms, a library, a restaurant, and a hotel, but a 1970s reno-vation did away with much of its original character. Herzog & de Meuron have sought to restore the architectural identity of the Volkshaus by remov-ing additions and 1970s cladding and finding ways to install modern technical services within the forms of the original building. They also designed a very contemporary version of the original Volk-shaus chair back that can be automatically indi-vidualized thanks to computer-aided production. As they point out: "It was important for us to work exclusively with quality materials like tin, leather, and wood, which acquire a patina through years of use. Striking architectural elements of 1925 have been reiterated elsewhere in various scales and articulations."

↑
A bar area near the street side of the restaurant. Black is the dominant color here.

↓
The entrance to the main dining room, which has a whiter tonality.

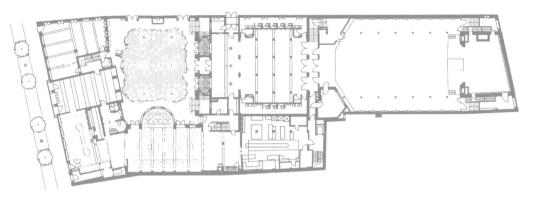

↑
A plan of the restaurant and the interior courtyard of the building, which is used as a Biergarten during the warmer months.

↓
Works of art mark the interior spaces in many different locations.

LEISURE

EDU CATION & RESEA RCH

UNIVERSIDADE AGOSTINHO NETO by PERKINS+WILL

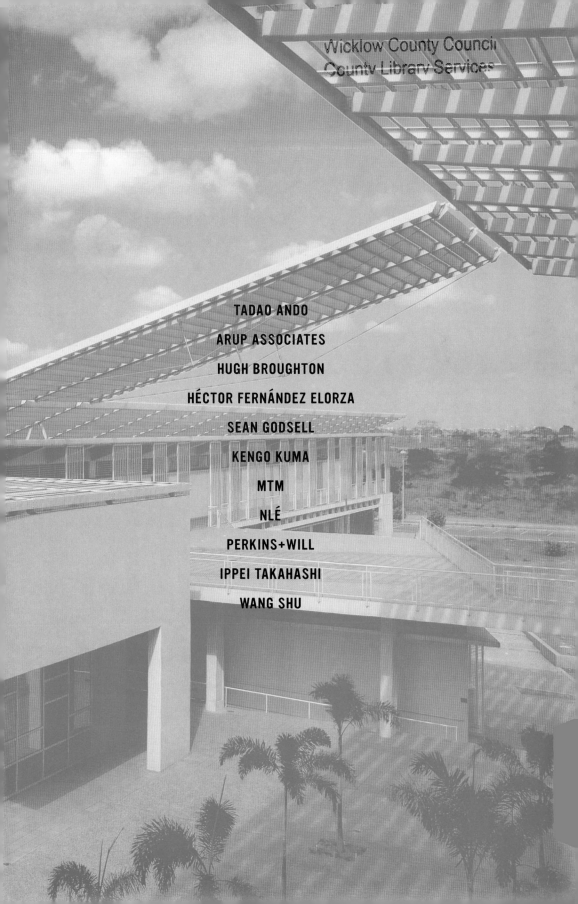

TADAO ANDO

ARUP ASSOCIATES

HUGH BROUGHTON

HÉCTOR FERNÁNDEZ ELORZA

SEAN GODSELL

KENGO KUMA

MTM

NLÉ

PERKINS+WILL

IPPEI TAKAHASHI

WANG SHU

CENTER FOR BIOMEDICAL RESEARCH OF ARAGON (CIBA)

2008–13

LOCATION Avda San Juan Bosco 13, 50009 Zaragoza, Spain, www.iacs.aragon.es
AREA 6062 m² — CLIENT Aragon Institute of Health Sciences (IACS) — COST €15 680 200
COLLABORATION Laura Casas, Alberto Palencia, Jorge Conde

Situated between an athletics track and a hospital, and near pedestrian access to the university campus, the steel and concrete Center for Biomedical Research presents ventilated façades with exterior insulation in which green and gray profiled steel sheet and anodized extruded aluminum slats have been employed, resulting in a passive energy system that obviates solar gain while allowing indirect natural light to enter. Further clarifying the design process, the architects say: "The development of the structure, following the north-south axis of the plot, leads us to adopt a filter-system for the whole façade that changes and vibrates (on the) different levels and becomes transparent or densifies according to the different viewpoints of users inside as much as of pedestrians outside." Three specialized circulation and installation cores are organized around a central nucleus while laboratory areas are buried in the ground and central access occurs at the upper level near the campus paths.

↑
Although it is relatively low and compact, the building stands out because of the undulations in its slatted façade.

←
The structure actually reveals almost nothing of its function nor indeed of its interior layout. Its skin appears to be dense or transparent according to viewpoints from within or from the outside.

→

An elevation drawing shows the irregular openings and use of the green color in different parts of the building. Similarly, interior volumes are varied according to their use without recourse to a strictly orthogonal layout.

↓

A conference room in the Center for Biomedical Research exudes an ordered and compact feeling that corresponds to the exterior appearance of the building.

CONSERVATORY OF MUSIC, DANCE, AND THEATER

2011–13

LOCATION 528 Avenue Mozart, 13100 Aix-en-Provence, France
AREA 7400 m² — CLIENT City of Aix-en-Provence — COST €16 million

This project includes a music school and an auditorium. Set on an irregular, sloping L-shaped site, the design aims to insert itself in a "biological" fashion into the old city. As the architects say, they did not choose to interrupt the complexity by inserting a minimal object in the old town, "but designed a membrane that responds variously like a creature's skin toward the intricate and diverse boundary state." Clad in anodized aluminum, this changing façade is compared to an alligator's skin, which ends up looking like a "musical score," while the school wing of the complex is a concrete structure and steel was employed for the auditorium wing.

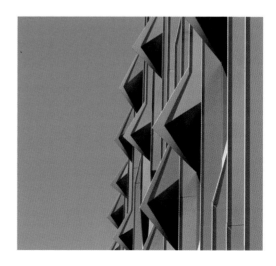

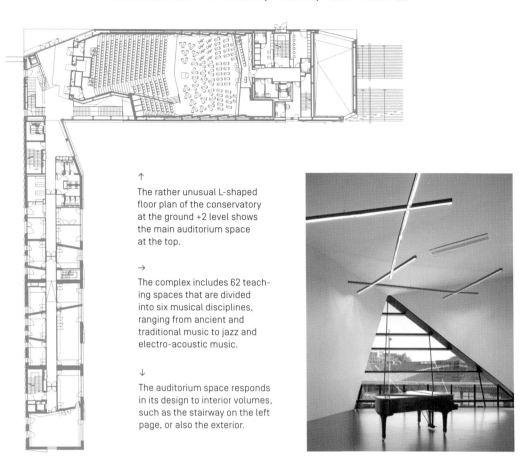

↑
The rather unusual L-shaped floor plan of the conservatory at the ground +2 level shows the main auditorium space at the top.

→
The complex includes 62 teaching spaces that are divided into six musical disciplines, ranging from ancient and traditional music to jazz and electro-acoustic music.

↓
The auditorium space responds in its design to interior volumes, such as the stairway on the left page, or also the exterior.

Héctor Fernández Elorza

FACULTY OF CELLULAR AND GENETIC BIOLOGY

2009–12

LOCATION Via G, s/n, UAH Campus, Alcalá de Henares, 28871 Madrid, Spain, www.uah.es
AREA 3150 m² — CLIENT University of Alcalá—UAH — COST €3.6 million
COLLABORATION Raúl García Cuevas, Ignacio Delgado Conde (Technical Architects), Montse Zamorano

The project involved the rehabilitation and extension of the Faculty of Cellular and Genetic Biology of the University of Alcalá—UAH. The existing building, a former military aerodrome structure, had to be both maintained and extended in order to adapt to the program: its concrete
structure was reinforced with metal, a fourth floor was added, and a polycarbonate façade was
set on the west side to bring natural light to corridors inside. The new concrete structure, to the
west, contains offices for the teaching staff and seminar and meeting rooms, and is linked to
the older building via connecting bridges that also bring light and ventilation to the central zone
of the new building. It stands on four piers and thick girders with cantilevers at the ends, permit-
ting visual connection from the common areas on the ground floor.

The architect juxtaposes such features as a polycarbonate-coated façade added to the older building with a calm, minimal approach, as seen below.

↑
A section drawing shows the new structure in the foreground and the older one, dating from the 1940s and renovated several times since, to the rear.

↓
The new concrete structure is seen in this image—a forceful exercise in equilibrium.

←
The projecting concrete planes
serve to protect interior spaces
from the sun, while also creating
an impression of levitation or lightness in the concrete structure.

This impression of weightlessness
can be seen in the images on
this page, where concrete and glass
form crisply defined volumes.

FACULTY OF ENGINEERING AND COMPUTING

2009–12

LOCATION 3 Gulson Road, Coventry CV1 2JH, UK, +44 24 77 65 88 88, www.coventry.ac.uk
AREA 15 500 m² — CLIENT Coventry University — COST €31.5 million — COLLABORATION
Vinci Construction (Main Contractor), Mero Schmidlin (Cladding Sub-Contractor)

This structure for Coventry University includes a high-performance engineering center with flight simulators and engine test cells; a high-precision wind tunnel testing facility; two lecture theaters that can be subdivided for conferences; collaborative classrooms for 4000 students, including IT workspaces; communal interactive spaces with learning booths; and integrated academic offices, the whole linked by a state-of-the-art communications backbone. The design places an emphasis on "proportion and mathematical beauty." Applying the theory of Harmonic Proportions, the architects made use of a perfect square for the outer boundary of the footprint, with an inner boundary in the shape of "a perfect Ptolemy's quadrilateral and with all primary line intersections being perfect harmonic ratios." The concrete structure includes steel to support the interactive zone façade, which is an anodized aluminum rain screen with timber mullions and veneered timber internal lining. The Faculty of Engineering and Computing achieved a BREEAM excellent rating for environmental sustainability.

←

The façade has anodized aluminum rain screens with timber mullions and a veneered timber internal lining.

↓

The building has a perfect square as the outer boundary of its footprint, while the inner boundary creates a perfect Ptolemy's quadrilateral with all primary line intersections conceived along perfect harmonic ratios.

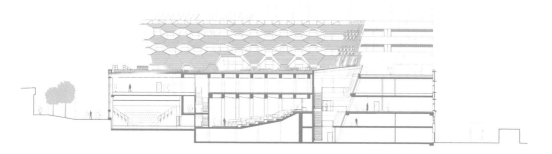

↑

The east-west section of the building.

↓

Interior spaces are both open and luminous everywhere, making it clear that engineering is very much a part not only of the studies here, but also of the architecture.

Hugh Broughton

HALLEY VI ANTARCTIC RESEARCH STATION

2007–13

LOCATION   latitude 75°35'S, longitude 26°39'W, www.antarctica.ac.uk/living_and_working/
research_stations/halley — AREA 1510 m² — CLIENT British Antarctic Survey
COST £25.855 million — COLLABORATION AECOM (Structure, Services, Fire, Acoustics),
Galliford Try International (Main Contractor)

The Halley Station—the most southerly research station of the British Antarctic Survey (BAS)—
was erected on a 150-meter-thick ice shelf that is moving toward the sea at a rate of 400 meters per year. Temperatures drop to -56˚C and winds blow in excess of 160 kilometers per hour;
access by ship and plane is limited to a three-month summer period. The competition-winning
scheme is intended to house 16 people in the winter and 52 in the summer, and to be easy to
build, operate, and dismantle. Given the rate of movement of the ice shelf, it was also required
that the station could be relocated inland if necessary. Finally it had to be set up above rising
snow levels. Built according to the Environmental Protocols of the Antarctic Treaty, the steel-

Designed for extreme weather conditions, the structure has to deal with high snow drifts and must be potentially moveable, whence its unusual appearance.

frame structure is aligned perpendicular to the prevailing winds so that snow drifts form on one side only and is clad with highly insulated, pre-glazed, painted, fiber-reinforced plastic (FRP) panels. Daylight simulating lamps and other design elements help the residents to weather the 105-day-long night of winter and heating is provided by a CHP plant controlled by BMS. Water usage has been cut from 120 liters per person per day at Halley V to 20 liters at Halley VI with a vacuum drainage system and low water-use devices. Sewage is treated in a bioreactor while sludge is incinerated and clean water effluent is returned to the ice.

←

A spiral staircase obviously saves space but also introduces a touch of elegance.

→

The stringent technical requirements of the building did not keep the architects from accentuating the quality of the design or convivial spaces like the room seen here.

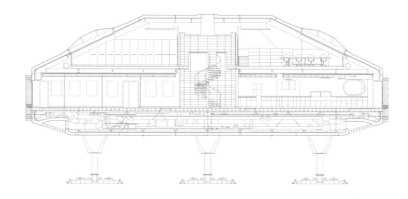

↑

A section of the Science Module with its central spiral staircase topped by a triple-glazed sky light.

→

Another section of the Science Module which has a painted GRP (a thin-shell glass reinforced plastic) cladding with PIR (Polyisocyanurate) closed cell foam insulation.

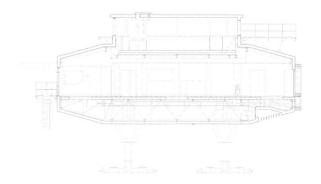

MAKOKO FLOATING SCHOOL

2012–13

LOCATION Makoko Community, Lagos, Nigeria
AREA 220 m²

Makoko Floating School is a prototype floating structure, built for the historic water community of Makoko, located on the lagoon of Nigeria's largest city, Lagos. This pilot project has taken an innovative approach to addressing the community's social and physical needs in view of the impact of climate change and a rapidly urbanizing African context. Its main aim is to generate a sustainable, ecological, alternative building system and to contribute to urban water culture for the large population of Africa's coastal regions. The low-cost, three-story, A-frame structure, which floats with the help of 250 plastic barrels, offers a 93-square-meter play area, classrooms, a rainwater collection system, and composting toilets. Designed for about 100 elementary-school children, the building, as *The New York Times* wrote, also "provides a flexible and robust prototype for housing and other potential structures."

The aim of the structure is nothing less
than to "generate a sustainable, ecological,
alternative building system for the local
urban water culture."

↑
The structure was built with wood, bamboo, and plastic barrels, and is 10 meters high with a 10×10 meter base.

↓
The open design rendered possible by the local climate also facilities communication and access from the 100 000 people of the Makoko waterfront community.

PLAZA MAYOR SERVICES BUILDING

2009–12

LOCATION UAM, Campus Cantoblanco, Calle Francisco Tomás y Valiente 5, 28031 Madrid, Spain, +34 914 97 51 00, www.uam.es — **AREA** 26725 m² — **CLIENT** Universidad Autónoma de Madrid **COST** €15.776 million — **COLLABORATION** Miguel García, Alberto Palencia, Jose A. Alonso

The Autonomous University of Madrid— generally known by its acronym UAM—is one of the top universities in Spain. The green boulevard and central space of the campus are the setting for the Plaza Mayor Services Building, which was designed as a "folded platform" around the "empty inside" of Plaza Mayor, with considerable emphasis placed on the project being seen as a prolongation of the natural landscape. From a parking area located above natural ground level, enriched with planted embankments, a sequence of covered paths created by generous cantilevered volumes, seven bridges, and communication towers intended as "urban milestones" invite visitors to discover the central plaza. The exterior enclosure of the square presents gray polycarbonate with embedded metallic resins while the interior enclosure is made of glass and a polycarbonate skin that is not touched by the interior partitioning in laminated glass. Various platforms contain the program spaces and the more uniform volumes are contrasted with blue, green, and golden colors.

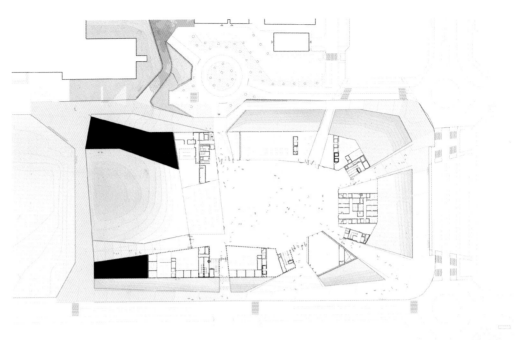

↑
The lower level plan of the Plaza Mayor shows the horseshoe or "folded" form of the services building that envelopes the actual square.

↓
The architects used elements such as concrete and steel but they succeed in imposing a feeling of lightness and transparency.

The architect Alberto Campo Baeza wrote of this project: "Here a landscape has been built and in its interior all the services (have been placed)."

Sean Godsell

RMIT DESIGN HUB

2007–12

LOCATION 150 Victoria Street, Carlton, Melbourne, VIC 3000, Australia, +61 3 9925 2041, www.designhub.rmit.edu.au — **AREA** 13 000 m² — **CLIENT** RMIT University **COLLABORATION** Peddle Thorp Architects (Architect of Record)

The RMIT Design Hub is intended for design research and postgraduate education in areas as diverse as fabric and fashion design, architecture, aeronautical engineering, industrial design, landscape architecture, and urban design. This brief clearly required "a high level of adaptability and flexibility." An exhibition space and design archive allows for interaction with the public, while lecture, seminar, and multipurpose rooms provide space for a wide variety of activities. Ecological concerns are addressed with such methods as water recycling, and large areas for photovoltaic cells. The façade has a double glazed inner skin on each face of the building and an automated operable second skin shading device. A secondary galvanized-steel frame is set out 700 millimeters from the curtain wall face of the building.

The façade consists in a double glazed inner skin on each face of the building and an automated, operable, second-skin shading device that surrounds the entire building.

←

The architect's sensitivity to color and light, combining a certain opacity or density with an awareness of the sun, is expressed with a variety of materials.

An exhibition space and design archive provide a public interface with the areas of industry and research. These spaces are combined with lecture, seminar, and multipurpose rooms.

ROBERTO GARZA SADA CENTER

2009–12

LOCATION Av. Ignacio Morones Prieto 4500 Pte., 66238 San Pedro Garza García,
Nuevo León, Mexico, +52 81 8215 1000, ext. 1500, www.udem.edu.mx/centrorobertogarzasada/
AREA 13 115 m² — CLIENT University of Monterrey

The Roberto Garza Sada Center is Tadao Ando's first public work in Latin America. The six-story reinforced-concrete building houses studios, laboratories, and teaching spaces for approximately 500 students of the Art, Architecture, and Design school of the University of Monterrey. As Tadao Ando explains, this project is linked to his House in Monterrey (2008–11): "It was Mrs. Fernandez, the grandmother of the client of the house and the daughter of Roberto Garza Sada, who approached me as a representative of the University and asked me to design the RGS Center." Set on a 20 700-square-meter site located on the northern side of the campus near the entrance to the University, the nine-meter-square grid plan is slightly angled to face the nearby Cumbres de Monterrey National Park. The complex is divided into three segments along the longitudinal axis with circulation concentrated in the central public zone. An atrium—dubbed the Gate of Creation—is carved out of the volume in what Tadao Ando calls "the main architectural concept" of the project. In his words, the atrium is "a void defined by two hyperbolic paraboloid shells excavated from a cuboid 99 meters wide, 27 meters deep, and 32.4 meters tall." The overall impression of the exposed concrete structure is one of solidity.

Though always known as a master of concrete, Tadao Ando has rarely ventured into forms as unexpected as the great arch seen above. Below, the central circulation void.

→
An axonometric
view of the building
with its stepped
public outdoor space.

↓
The powerful archi-
tecture is everywhere
present, but the
ultimate goal of the
design is to foster
creative exchange.

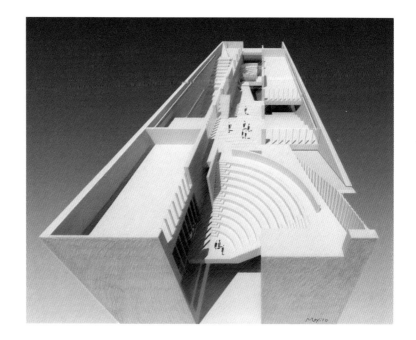

↑

As has almost always been the case, Tadao Ando makes masterful use of light and shadow, here accentuated by the strong Mexican sun and the depths of shadow imposed by the powerful concrete forms.

The stepped section of a circle forms an interior void opening to the spectacular mountain scenery of Monterrey.

Ippei Takahashi

SHICHIGAHAMA TOHYAMA NURSERY

2012–13

LOCATION Shichigahama, Miyagi, Japan — AREA 977 m² — CLIENT Municipality of Shichigahama — COST ¥230.475 million — COLLABORATION Konishi Structural Engineers (Structure), Kankyo Engineering (Mechanical and Electrical)

Ippei Takahashi was selected for this reconstruction project for a public nursery damaged by the 2011 Tohoku earthquake and tsunami through a design competition designating Shichigahama Tohyama Nursery as "a leading project for creative restoration in Shichigahama." A single-story building measuring nearly 1000 square meters surrounds an open schoolyard of the same dimensions. The aim of the low horizontal design is to integrate the structure with its natural environment, allowing children to run around freely both inside and outside, and avoid any feeling of oppression. The architect explains that "the outer part has a diverse range of spaces arranged like a village through a series of workshops, and serves a wide range of needs...."
A meeting area is located at the entrance to allow local residents to meet and communicate in a friendly environment and a number of open-air spaces and loggias face the courtyard. Takahashi feels that "on the whole, this building can be seen as a town garden or park, rather than a mere nursery school." Based on a galvanized-steel frame, the exterior walls of the structure are 3-millimeter steel sheet. The painting in the pool is by the artist Tomoko Nagai (Tomio Koyama Gallery).

Everything in the design, from its single-level
height to the reflective metal cladding, is intended
to give a modest impression, or almost of an
absence of architecture.

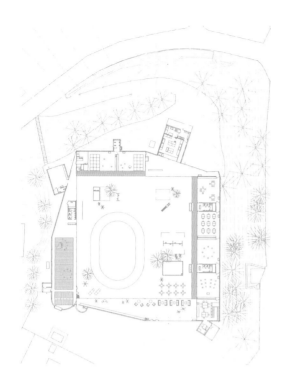

←

A site plan of the facility, with a field and small pool nearly encircled by the single-story structures forming the nursery

↓

The intentionally natural environment allows children to feel free while they are protected by the configuration of the architecture itself.

Wang Shu

TILES HILL

2011–13

LOCATION Hangzhou, China — **AREA** 4680 m² — **CLIENT** China Academy of Art
COST $9.1 million — **COLLABORATION** Lu Wenyu, Chen Lichao

This is a supplementary facility intended for housing and visitor accommodation located on the Xiangshan campus designed by Wang Shu in Hangzhou. Inspired by the tile roofs of a village the architect visited 20 years ago in Hunan Province, Tiles Hill has a 120-meter-long tile roof, while 30 rammed-earth walls divide the building into six independent units: a teahouse, conference center, restaurant, and three courtyard hotels. A concrete frame was used to further strengthen the 60-centimeter-thick rammed-earth walls in order to respect earthquake resistance rules. The architect describes the project in the following words: "Viewed from the east and west, the building looks like a hill, with twists and turns. Viewed from the south and north, it looks like a hill-shaped ventilating screen; people can see through the building so that its volume is visually reduced. The structure resembles a small group of buildings overshadowed by a huge shed. The double roof not only keeps out the heat in summer but also generates impressive space. In rainy seasons, people can easily live under this shed and walk around quite freely."

↑
Section drawings of the complex give the impression of a series of related, interconnected volumes, almost forming a hillside landscape.

The tile roofs can be readily admired from the elevated walkway that spans across them, seen here on the bottom of both pages.

→

A view of the western hotel courtyard inspired by the Ningbo Tengtou Pavilion of the 2010 Shanghai Expo, also designed by Wang Shu (following spread).

↑
Under the 120-meter-long tile roof designed by the architect, pine wood bars form a large-span open space.

↓
The underside of one of the curving roofs.

The complex contains a teahouse, conference center, restaurant, and three courtyard-type hotels.

UNIVERSIDADE AGOSTINHO NETO

2002-11

LOCATION Luanda, Angola, www.uan.ao — **AREA** 35 000 m² (Phase 1) — **CLIENT** Ministry of Urban Affairs and Public Works on behalf of the Ministry of Education and the Universidade Agostinho Neto — **COST** $175 million (Phase 1) — **COLLABORATION** Dar Al-Handasah (Shair & Partners), Battle McCarthy Engineers (Phase 1)

Set on a 2000-hectare campus southeast of the Angolan capital, Luanda, this university is intended for up to 40 000 students in 12 faculties and four core departments. Perkins+Will developed a master plan for the project in 2000 (updated in 2009), and has already completed Phase 1 of the project (published here), which "forms the University's central academic core: buildings for faculties of chemistry, mathematics, physics, and computer sciences; and a central library and plaza." The central library plaza was designed as the heart of the campus and main gathering space. Canopies, elevated walkways, strategically ventilated space, and building masses are intended to facilitate airflow throughout. Future development will include expansion of academic facilities, administration, student residences, food service, sports fields and facilities, a research zone, student union, and conference center, many of which have already been tendered.

↑
The classroom bars
are simple concrete
structures with short
east-west façades
and long north-south
façades facing the
prevailing winds off
the Atlantic.

Louvered roof elements
covers portions of the
courtyards between the
bars, creating a series
of outdoor shaded gath-
ering spaces.

↑
The shape and angle of the roofs was calibrated using fluid dynamics modeling to create pressure differentiation across the bars, maximizing airflow in the manner of an airplane wing.

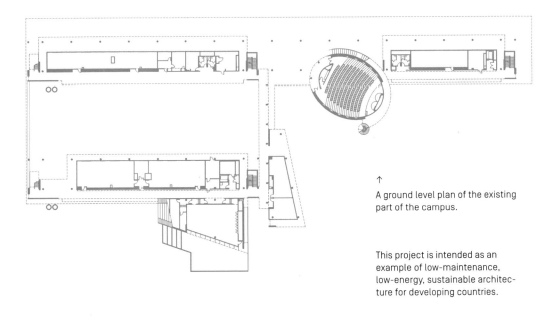

↑
A ground level plan of the existing part of the campus.

This project is intended as an example of low-maintenance, low-energy, sustainable architecture for developing countries.

EDUCATION & RESEARCH

AR CHI TEC TS

3XN → pp.158, 386

3XN A/S
Kanonbådsvej 8
1437 Copenhagen
Denmark

Tel: +45 70 26 26 48
Fax: +45 70 26 26 49
E-mail: 3xn@3xn.dk
Web: www.3xn.com

KIM HERFORTH NIELSEN was born in Sønderborg, Denmark, in 1954 and graduated from the Aarhus School of Architecture in 1981. He is the founder, Principal Partner, and Artistic Director of 3XN. The three other Partners of the firm are JAN AMMUNDSEN [Head of Competitions], BO BOJE LARSEN, and KASPER GULDAGER JENSEN, who is also the Director of GXN, the firm's innovation unit established in 2007. Recent work includes Ørestad College [Copenhagen, 2007]; the Saxo Bank [Copenhagen, 2008]; Horten Headquarters [Copenhagen, 2009]; Middelfart Savings Bank [Middelfart, 2010]; Bella Sky Hotel [Copenhagen, 2011]; Museum of Liverpool [Liverpool, UK, 2011]; Plassen Cultural Center [Molde, Norway, 2012]; the Buen Cultural Center [Mandal, Norway, 2012]; the Blue Planet [Kastrup, 2010–13, see p. 386]; and UN City [Copenhagen, 2010–14, see p. 158]. Current work includes the Copenhagen Arena [2016] and Station City Stockholm [Sweden, 2017], all in Denmark unless stated otherwise stated.

A-LAB → pp.142, 172

a-lab [Arkitekturlaboratoriet AS]
Drammensveien 130
0277 Oslo
Norway

Tel: +47 22 12 22 63
E-mail: office@a-lab.no
Web: www.a-lab.no

A-lab was founded in 2000 by two Partners, Geir Haaversen and Odd Klev. GEIR HAAVERSEN was born in 1977. He worked with Dark Arkitekter [1994–99] and at Bowim-Fuglo-Svingen [1999–2000], before becoming a Partner in a-lab [2000] and then the firm's Managing Director [2009].
ODD KLEV was born in 1969 and also has a degree in Architecture, obtained in Norway. He worked with Dark Arkitekter [1995–99] too, then at Lund

Hagem Architects [1999–2000], before becoming a founding Partner in a-lab in 2000. The firm currently employs 42 architects, a project administrator, and a marketing coordinator. Their work includes the AKS—Arctic Cultural Center [Hammerfest, 2004–08, see p. 172]; and the Statoil Regional and International Offices [Fornebu, 2010–12, see p. 142]; Søgne Town Hall and Library [Søgne, 2008–13]; a border crossing post [Sør-Varanger, 2010–14]; offices in the Barcode project, which they are involved in with Dark Arkitekter and MVRDV [Bjørvika, Oslo, 2014–16]; and the Flesland Business Park [Bergen, 2013–], all in Norway.

TADAO ANDO → p.446

Tadao Ando Architect & Associates
Osaka
Japan

Born in Osaka in 1941, TADAO ANDO was self-educated as an architect, largely through his travels in the United States, Europe, and Africa [1962–69]. He founded Tadao Ando Architect & Associates in Osaka in 1969. He has received the Alvar Aalto Medal, Finnish Association of Architects [1985]; the Medaille d'or, French Academy of Architecture [1989]; the 1992 Carlsberg Prize; and the 1995 Pritzker Prize. Notable recent buildings include the Modern Art Museum of Fort Worth [Fort Worth, Texas, USA, 1999–2002]; Chichu Art Museum on the Island of Naoshima in the Inland Sea [Japan, 2004]; Omote Sando Hills complex [Tokyo, Japan, 2006]; 21_21 Design Sight [Tokyo, Japan, 2004–07]; Tokyu Toyoko Line Shibuya Station [Shibuya, Tokyo, Japan, 2006–08]; and the renovation of the Punta della Dogana [Venice, Italy, 2007–09]. Ando has recently completed the WSJ-352 Building on the Novartis Campus [Basel, Switzerland, 2004–10]; the Stone Sculpture Museum [Bad Münster am Stein, Germany, 2010]; Château la Coste Art Center [Le Puy-Sainte-Réparade, France, 2008–11]; the Roberto Garza Sada Center [University of Monterrey, Monterrey, Mexico, 2009–12, see p. 446]; the Ando Museum [Naoshima, Kawaga, Japan, 2012–13]; the Clark Art and Conservation Center [Williamstown, Massachusetts, USA, 2006–14]; and the Shanghai Poly Theater [Shanghai, China, 2014]. He is working on the Abu Dhabi Maritime Museum [Abu Dhabi, UAE, 2006–].

WIEL ARETS → pp.74, 92

Wiel Arets Architects [WAA]
D'Artagnanlaan 29
6213 CH Maastricht
The Netherlands

Tel: +31 43 351 22 00
Fax: +31 43 321 21 92
E-mail: info@wielaretsarchitects.com
Web: www.wielaretsarchitects.com

WIEL ARETS was born in Heerlen, the Netherlands, in 1955. He graduated from the Technical University in Eindhoven in 1983, and established Wiel Arets Architect & Associates in Heerlen the following year, moving to Maastricht in 1996. The firm has recently been reorganized as Wiel Arets Architects [WAA]. Arets's interest in architectural theory led him to cofound the magazine *Wiederhall* in 1987. Arets was Dean of the Berlage Institute, Postgraduate Laboratory of Architecture in Amsterdam [1995–98], and has been Dean of the Illinois Institute of Technology College Architecture since the fall of 2012. Built work of the firm includes the Academy of Art and Architecture [Maastricht, 1989–93]; 67 apartments [Tilburg, 1992–94]; the AZL Pension Fund Headquarters [Heerlen, 1990–95]; a police station in Vaals [1993–96]; the Lensvelt Factory and Office [Breda, 1999–2000]; and the Utrecht University Library [UBU, Utrecht, 1997–2004]. More recently, the firm has worked on Jellyfish House [Marbella, Spain, 2013, see p. 74]; V House [Maastricht, the Netherlands, 2013, see p. 92]; the Allianz Headquarters [Zurich, Switzerland, 2008–14]; Regiocentrale Zuid [Maasbracht, 2008–14]; and Amsterdam Centraal Station IJhal [Amsterdam, 2010–15], all in the Netherlands unless otherwise indicated.

ARUP ASSOCIATES → p.420

Arup Associates
8 Fitzroy Street
London W1T 4BJ
UK

Tel: +44 20 77 55 21 97
E-mail: info@arupassociates.com
Web: www.arupassociates.com

Arup Associates is the integrated design studio of the multinational consulting engineering group Arup. Started by Sir Ove Arup [1895–1988] in 1963, the studio practices multi-disciplinary design where engineers and architects work side by side in embedded teams in a single practice. The practice is currently led by the architect DECLAN O'CARROLL (born in 1963 in Burnley) and the building environmental engineer MICHAEL BEAVEN (born in 1965). Recent work by the firm includes the Qatar Showcase (Doha, Qatar, 2010); BSkyB Studios (West London, UK, 2007–11); the Faculty of Engineering and Computing, Coventry University (Coventry, UK, 2009–12, see p. 420); Druk White Lotus School (Ladakh, Northern India, 2002–14); the Singapore Sports Hub (Singapore, 2010–14); and King Abdullah Sports City (KASC, Jeddah, Saudi Arabia, 2011–14).

ASYMPTOTE → p.330

Asymptote Architecture
11–45 46th Avenue
Long Island City, New York
NY 11101, USA

Tel: +1 212 343 7333
Fax: +1 718 937 3320
E-mail: info@asymptote.net
Web: www.asymptote.net

HANI RASHID received his B.Arch degree from Carlton University and a M.Arch degree from the Cranbrook Academy of Art, Bloomfield Hills, Michigan. LISE ANNE COUTURE received her B.Arch degree from Carlton University, Canada, and her M.Arch degree from Yale University. They are cofounders and Principals of Asymptote Architecture, founded in New York in 1988. In 2004 Rashid and Couture received the Frederick Kiesler Prize for their body of work spanning the disciplines of Architecture and Art. Asymptote's built works include the HydraPier, a public cultural building housing technology and art located near Schipol Airport (Haarlemmermeer, the Netherlands, 2002); the Carlos Miele Flagship Store on West 14th Street in Manhattan (New York, New York, USA, 2003); the design of the 2004 Venice Biennale of Architecture, "Metamorph" (Italy); the Alessi Flagship Store in the SoHo area of Manhattan and 166 Perry Street condominium in Manhattan (New York, New York, USA, 2006); the Yas Hotel (Abu Dhabi, UAE, 2008–09); and the ARC—River Culture Multimedia Theater (Daegu, South Korea, 2012, see p. 330).

BERNARDO BADER → p.230

Bernardo Bader Architects
Steinebach 11, Dornbirn
6850 Vorarlberg, Austria

Tel: +43 55 72 20 78 96
E-mail: mail@bernardobader.com
Web: www.bernardobader.com

Born in 1974 in Krumbach, Austria, BERNARDO BADER studied architecture at the University of Innsbruck (1993–2001). He received a degree in Engineering from that institution in 2001. He worked at Feichtinger Architectes (Paris, 1998–99). He created his own office in Dornbirn in 2003 and officially became an Austrian civil engineer in 2006. Recent work by Bernardo Bader includes the Islamic Cemetery (Altach, 2010–11, see p. 230), which received a 2013 Aga Khan Award for Architecture; the Saunahouse (Koblach, 2012); the Municipal Center (Steinberg am Rofan, 2013); Fontanella House (Fontanella, 2013); the Austrian Embassy (Zagreb, Croatia, 2013); Susi-Weigel Kindergarden (Bludenz, 2013); and House on the Moor (Krumbach, 2013), all in Austria unless otherwise indicated.

SHIGERU BAN → p.123

Shigeru Ban Architects
5-2-4 Matsubara
Setagaya
Tokyo 156–0043
Japan

Tel: +81 3 3324 6760
Fax: +81 3 3324 6789
E-mail: tokyo@shigerubanarchitects.com
Web: www.shigerubanarchitects.com

Born in 1957 in Tokyo, SHIGERU BAN studied at SCI-Arc from 1977 to 1980. He then attended the Cooper Union School of Architecture, where he studied under John Hejduk (1980–82). He worked in the office of Arata Isozaki (1982–83), before founding his own firm in Tokyo in 1985. He designed the Japanese Pavilion at Expo 2000 in Hannover. His work includes the Nicolas G. Hayek Center (Tokyo, Japan, 2007); the Paper Teahouse (London, UK, 2008); Quinta Botanica (Algarve, Portugal, 1999/2004–09); Haesley Nine Bridges Golf Clubhouse (Yeoju, South Korea, 2009); the Paper Tube Tower (London, UK, 2009); and the Metal Shutter Houses on West 19th Street

in New York (New York, USA, 2010). He installed his Paper Temporary Studio on top of the Pompidou Center in Paris to work on the new Centre Pompidou-Metz (Metz, France, 2010). Recent work includes the Camper Pavilion (Alicante, Spain; Sanya, China; Miami, Florida, USA; Lorient, France, 2011); Kobe Kushinoya (Osaka, Japan, 2011); L'Aquila Temporary Concert Hall (L'Aquila, Italy, 2011); Container Temporary Housing, disaster relief project for the east Japan earthquake and tsunami (Miyagi, Japan, 2011); Tamedia (Zurich, Switzerland, 2011–13); and Cardboard Cathedral (Christchurch, New Zealand, 2013, see p. 184). Current work includes the Swatch Group Headquarters and Production Facility (Bienne, Switzerland, 2012–16); and the Cité Musicale (Ile Séguin, Boulogne-Billancourt, France, 2016).

BERCY CHEN → p.44

Bercy Chen Studio LP
1111 East 11th Street, Suite 200
Austin, TX 78702, USA

Tel: +1 512 481 0092
E-mail: info@bcarc.com
Web: www.bcarc.com

THOMAS BERCY was born in Belgium. He attended the Beaux-Arts school in Brussels, where he studied four years in the fine arts program and two years in the architecture program. He then studied at the University of Texas at Austin, where he graduated with a B.A. in Architecture (1999) and a B.A. in Architectural Engineering (2000). He also studied abroad in the Urbanism program at the Pontificia Universidad Catolica de Santiago. He returned to Belgium to join Samyn and Partners, and in 2000 he moved to Austin, Texas, where he started work at M. J. Neal Architects. CALVIN CHEN was born in Taipei, Taiwan, in 1974. He moved with his family to Brisbane, Australia, in 1989 and attended St. Peter's Lutheran College. He graduated in 1998 from the University of Texas at Austin with a B.A. in Architecture. He formed Bercy Chen Studio LP with Thomas Bercy in 2001. Recent work includes the Medicine Wheel House (Austin, 2011); Edgeland House (Austin, 2011–12, see p. 44); Oak Creek Village, Phase 1 (Austin, 2012); Becoming Forest (Sunset Valley House (Austin, 2013); Enfield Residence (Austin, 2013); West Lake House (Austin, 2013); Ranch House (Fredericksburg,

2013); Eco Resort [Pedernales, 2013]; Zero Space Museum [Austin, 2013]; and ChaiOne Headquarters [Houston, 2013], all in Texas, USA.

THIAGO BERNARDES → p. 56

Bernardes Arquitetura
Rua Corcovado 250, Jardim Botânico
Rio de Janeiro, RJ 22460–050, Brazil

Tel: +55 21 2512 7743
E-mail: contato@bernardesarq.com
Web: www.bernardesarquitetura.com.br

THIAGO BERNARDES was born in Rio de Janeiro in 1974. His grandfather was Sergio Bernardes, a Brazilian architect who won Brussels' International Fair's prize in 1958. His father was Claudio Bernardes, founder-Partner of Claudio Bernardes + Jacobsen Arquitetura in Rio. In 1992, he entered Santa Ursula College in Rio, but preferred to engage in a self-taught career. In 1994, he opened his first office with Miguel Pinto Guimarães, developing more than 30 residential projects between 1996 and 2001. Subsequent to his father's death, he and his Partner associated themselves with Paulo Jacobsen and created a new office. In 2011, Thiago Bernardes again preferred to start a new firm, along with CAMILA TARIKI, MARCIA SANTORO, DANTE FURLAN, and NUNO COSTA NUNES, founding Bernardes Arquitetura. They currently have a team of 60 people with offices in Rio de Janeiro and São Paulo. The firm's work includes the AB House [Abu Dhabi, UAE, 2012]; AK House [Angra dos Reis, Rio de Janeiro, 2012]; GCP House [Porto Feliz, São Paulo, 2012–13, see p. 56]; Gávea House [Rio de Janeiro, 2013]; RGB House [Itacaré, Bahia, 2013]; and the CF House [Porto Feliz, São Paulo, 2013], all in Brazil unless stated otherwise.

BERNARDES + JACOBSEN → p. 270

Bernardes Arquitetura
Rua Corcovado 250, Jardim Botânico
Rio de Janeiro, RJ 22460–050, Brazil

Tel: +55 21 2512 7743
E-mail: contato@bernardesarq.com
Web: www.bernardesarquitetura.com.br

Jacobsen Arquitetura
Rua Pacheco Leão 862
Jardim Botânico
Rio de Janeiro, RJ 22460–030, Brazil

Tel/Fax: +55 21 227 42700
E-mail:
contato@jacobsenarquitetura.com
Web: www.jacobsenarquitetura.com

THIAGO BERNARDES was born in Rio de Janeiro in 1974. The office of Bernardes + Jacobsen was created in 1980 by his father, Claudio Bernardes, and Paulo Jacobsen, pioneers of a new type of residential architecture based on an effort to combine contemporary design and Brazilian culture. Thiago Bernardes worked in his father's office from 1991 to 1996, when he left to create his own firm, working on more than 30 residential projects between that date and 2001. With the death of his father, Thiago Bernardes reintegrated the firm and began to work with PAULO JACOBSEN, who was born in 1954 in Rio. Jacobsen studied photography in London before graduating from the Bennett Methodist Institute in 1979. BERNARDO JACOBSEN was born in 1980 and joined the company in 2007, after graduating from the Federal University of Rio de Janeiro and working in the offices of Christian de Portzamparc and Shigeru Ban. Some of their significant projects include the Gerdau Headquarters [Porto Alegre, 2005]; FW House [Guaruja, 2005]; and the MPM Agency Main Office [São Paulo, 2006]. More recent work includes the JH House [São Paulo, 2008]; the JZ House [Bahia, 2008]; RW House [Búzios, 2009]; the FN and DB Houses [both in São Paulo, 2009]; and the Joá House [Rio de Janeiro, 2010–11], all in Brazil unless stated otherwise. Finally, they worked together on MAR, Art Museum of Rio [Rio de Janeiro, 2010–13, see p. 270]. The office split in 2011, creating Jacobsen Arquitetura (Bernardo and Paulo Jacobsen) and Bernardes Arquitetura.

BIG → p. 276

BIG, Bjarke Ingels Group
Kløverbladsgade 56, 2500 Valby
Denmark

Tel: +45 72 21 72 27
E-mail: big@big.dk
Web: www.big.dk

BJARKE INGELS was born in 1974 in Copenhagen, Denmark. He graduated from the Royal Academy of Arts School of Architecture [Copenhagen, 1999] and attended the ETSAB School of Architecture [Barcelona]. He created

his own office in 2005 under the name Bjarke Ingels Group [BIG], after having cofounded PLOT Architects in 2001 and collaborated with Rem Koolhaas at OMA [Rotterdam]. In 2004 he was awarded the Golden Lion at the Venice Biennale for the Stavanger Concert House. One of his latest completed projects, the Mountain [Copenhagen, Denmark, 2006–08], has received numerous awards. BIG is led by Partners Bjarke Ingels, Andreas Klok Pedersen, Finn Nørkjær, David Zahle, Jakob Lange, and Thomas Christoffersen and Managing Partners Sheela Maini Søgaard and Kai-Uwe Bergmann, and has offices in Copenhagen and New York. Recent work includes the Danish Expo Pavilion [Shanghai, China, 2010]; the Superkilen Master Plan [Copenhagen, Denmark, 2011]; the Maritime Museum of Denmark [Helsingør, Denmark, 2007–13, see p. 276]; and the renovation and expansion of the Kimball Art Center [Park City, Utah, USA, 2013–15]. Ongoing work includes the Amager Bakke Waste-to-Energy Plant [Copenhagen, Denmark, 2009–]; the Shenzhen International Energy Mansion [Shenzhen, China, 2013–]; and the Faroe Islands Education Center [Thorshavn, Faroe Islands, 2014–].

TATIANA BILBAO → p. 32

Tatiana Bilbao S.C.
Paseo de la Reforma 382–301
Colonia Juárez
Delegación Cuauhtémoc
06600 Mexico City, Mexico

Tel/Fax: +52 55 8589 8822
E-mail: info@tatianabilbao.com
Web: www.tatianabilbao.com

TATIANA BILBAO was born in Mexico City in 1972. She graduated in Architecture and Urbanism from the Universidad Iberoamericana in 1996. She was an Advisor for Urban Projects at the Urban Housing and Development Department of Mexico City [1998–99]. In 2004, she created Tatiana Bilbao S.C., with projects in China, Spain, France, and Mexico, and also became a Professor of Design at the Universidad Iberoamericana. Her office was selected as one of the top 10 emerging firms in the 2007 Architectural Record Design Vanguard. In 2010, two new Partners, David Vaner and Catia Bilbao, joined her firm. She curated the Ruta del Peregrino [with Derek Dellekamp], a 117-kilometer pilgrimage route where numerous architects created stopping points and small buildings (Route of the Pilgrim), from Ameca to Talpa de Allende (Jalisco, 2009–11). Her built work includes Casa Ventura (Monterrey, 2010–11, see p. 32); Ajijic House (Chapala Lake, Jalisco, 2011); Villa Ventura (Monterrey, 2011–12); Ciudadela, offices and headquarters of the National Library of Mexico (Mexico City, 2012); B3, B7, and B8—three housing complexes in the "Ilot A3" project (Lyon, France, 2013–18); and the Culiacán Botanical Garden (Culiacán, Sinaloa, 2011–). Ongoing work includes Veracruz Towers (Veracruz, 2011–); and Casa Demialma (Jolutia, Guerrero, 2011–), all in Mexico unless stated otherwise.

HUGH BROUGHTON → p. 424

Hugh Broughton Architects
41A Beavor Lane
London W6 9BL, UK

Tel: +44 20 87 35 99 59
E-mail: info@hbarchitects.co.uk
Web: www.hbarchitects.co.uk

HUGH BROUGHTON was born in 1965 in Worcester, UK. He attended the University of Edinburgh (1984–90) and obtained an M.A. Diploma in Architecture, RIBA. He worked with Manser Associates (1987–88) and with Troughton McAslan (1990–94), before setting up his own office in London in 1995. Hugh Broughton won the 2005 competition to design the first fully relocatable research base—the Halley VI Antarctic Research Station (Brunt Ice Shelf, Antarctica, 2007–13, see p. 424)—and has subsequently received other, similar commissions for an Antarctic research station for Spain (South Shetland Islands) and an atmospheric laboratory for the United States on the Greenland Ice Cap. Although now considered a leading practice in polar designs, the firm has also completed the British Council South East Asia HQ (Kuala Lumpur, Malaysia, 2002); Maidstone Museum East Wing (Maidstone, 2010–12); and the Royal Society of Chemistry Refurbishment (London, 2011). Aside from the ongoing work for extreme climates, Hugh Broughton is presently working on the Institution of Structural Engineers HQ (London, 2014–15); the Henry Moore Foundation Visitor Center and Archive (Perry Green, 2015–16); and the Gallery for the Portland Collection (Welbeck, 2014–16), all in the UK unless stated otherwise.

CARTER + BURTON → p. 50

Carter + Burton Architecture, PLC
11 West Main Street
Berryville, VA 22611, USA

Tel: +1 540 955 1644
Fax: +1 540 955 0410
E-mail: info@carterburton.com
Web: www.carterburton.com

PAGE CARTER attended the University of Virginia (1975–79), and Harvard GSD, where she obtained her M.Arch degree in 1987. She worked in several offices in Boston, Cambridge, Houston (Skidmore, Owings & Merrill), and Baltimore (RTKL), before founding Carter + Burton Architecture. JIM BURTON received a B.A. in Architecture from Mississippi State University (1990). He worked for several civil engineering and architecture firms and experimented with design-build projects (Studio Loggerheads, Virginia), before forming Carter + Burton in 1999. Their work includes Matoaka (Clarke County, 1999); the Shenandoah Retreat (Warren County, 2003); Yoga Studio (Clarke County, 2007); Boxhead (Clarke County, 2008); Barns of Rose Hill (Berryville, 2010); and Elk Run Ridge (Churchville, Augusta County, 2012, see p. 50), all in Virginia, USA.

MARCO CASAGRANDE → p. 334

Casagrande Laboratory
Puolukkakatu 4A
10300 Karjaa, Finland

Tel: +358 45 863 73 70
E-mail: info@clab.fi
Web: www.clab.fi

Born in 1971 in Turku, Finland, MARCO CASAGRANDE attended the Helsinki University of Technology, Department of Architecture. He worked in the office of Casagrande & Rintala (1998–2003). Casagrande is the Principal of Ruin Academy (Taiwan, Italy), an independent multidisciplinary research center, Casagrande Laboratory architects based in Finland, and WEAK!, together with Roan Ching-Yueh and Hsieh Ying-Chun, in Taiwan. His work includes Floating Sauna (Rosendal, Norway, 2002); Treasure Hill (Taipei, Taiwan, 2003); Post-Industrial Fleet (Venice Biennale, Italy, 2004); 7-Eleven Sauna (Taipei, Taiwan, 2007); Chen House (Sanjhih, Taiwan, 2008); Guandu River City (Taipei, Taiwan, 2009); and the Bug Dome (Shenzhen and Hong Kong Bi-City Biennale of Architecture/Urbanism, Shenzhen, China, 2009). More recently he completed Cicade (Taipei, Taiwan, 2011); and Sandworm (Beaufort Triennial of Contemporary Art, Belgium 2012). Marco Casagrande says that a ruin emerges when something "manmade has become part of nature. I am looking forward," he says "to designing ruins." His Ultra Ruin (Taipei City, Taiwan, 2013) is published here, see p. 334.

DAVID CHIPPERFIELD → pp. 284, 314

David Chipperfield Architects Ltd.
11 York Road, London SE1 7NX, UK

Tel: +44 20 76 20 48 00
Fax: +44 20 76 20 48 01
E-mail: info@davidchipperfield.co.uk
Web: www.davidchipperfield.com

Born in London in 1953, DAVID CHIPPERFIELD obtained his Diploma in Architecture from the Architectural Association (London, 1977). He worked in the offices of Norman Foster and Richard Rogers, before establishing David Chipperfield Architects (London, 1985). The firm now has offices in London, Berlin, Milan, and Shanghai. Built work includes the River and Rowing Museum (Henley-on-Thames, UK, 1989–97); Des Moines Public Library (Des Moines, Iowa, USA, 2002–06); the Museum of Modern Literature (Marbach am Neckar, Germany, 2002–06); the America's Cup Building "Veles et Vents" (Valencia, Spain, 2005–06); the Liangzhu Museum (Liangzhu Cultural Village, China, 2003–07); the Neues Museum (Museum Island, Berlin, Germany, 1997–2009); the City of Justice Law Courts (Barcelona, Spain, 2002–09); and the Anchorage Museum at Rasmuson Center (Anchorage, Alaska, USA, 2003–09). Recently the office has completed Museum Folkwang (Essen, Germany, 2007–10); the Kaufhaus Tyrol Department Store (Innsbruck, Austria, 2007–10); the Hepworth Gallery (Wakefield, UK, 2003–11); Turner Contemporary (Margate, UK, 2006–11); the Peek & Cloppenburg Flagship Store (Vienna, Austria, 2006–11); the expansion of the St. Louis Art Museum (St. Louis, Missouri, USA, 2009–13; see p. 314); and the Museo Jumex (Mexico City, Mexico, 2012–13, see p. 284). Underway is the Ansaldo City of Cultures (Milan, Italy, 2000–); and the Amorepacific Headquarters (Seoul, South Korea, 2017).

MANUEL CLAVEL-ROJO → p.196

Clavel Arquitectos, Peligros 3, 3ªA
30001 Murcia, Spain

Tel: +34 968 21 23 14
Fax: +34 968 97 01 19
E-mail: clavel-arquitectos@clavel-arquitectos.com
Web: www.clavel-arquitectos.com

MANUEL CLAVEL-ROJO was born in Murcia in 1976. He received his degree in Architecture from the Polytechnic University of Madrid. He served as head of Culture for the Murcia Architects Association (2007–10). He has been a Visiting Professor at Miami University (Florida) since 2012. His work includes the Las Salinas Marina (San Pedro del Pinatar, Murcia, 2002); Mesa del Castillo Hospital (Murcia, 2004); Portman Bay Regeneration Project (Portman, La Unión, 2007); Café del Arco (Murcia, 2009); Cloud Pantheon (Murcia, 2010, see p. 196); Avenida Libertad Parking Lot (Murcia, 2010); Casanueva Pharmacy (Murcia, 2010); Centrifugal Ultralight Pavilion (Shenzhen, China, 2011); rehabilitation of a penthouse for art collectors (Murcia, 2011); Liuye Lake Civic Center (Changde, Hunan, China, 2012); and the 4 in 1 House (Guadalupe, Murcia, 2013), all in Spain unless otherwise indicated.

PRESTON SCOTT COHEN → p.324

Preston Scott Cohen, Inc.
77 Pleasant Street
Cambridge, MA 02139, USA

Tel: +1 617 441 2110
Fax: +1 617 441 2113
E-mail: info@pscohen.com
Web: www.pscohen.com

Born in 1961, PRESTON SCOTT COHEN received his B.Arch degree from the Rhode Island School of Design (1983) and his M.Arch degree from the Harvard GSD (1985). Cohen is the Chair and Gerald M. McCue Professor of Architecture at Harvard GSD. Recent projects include the Goldman Sachs Arcade Canopy (New York, New York, USA, 2005–08); the Tel Aviv Museum of Art Amir Building (Israel, 2007–11), which was awarded the 2011 Design Review Award and the 2012 Time and Leisure Best Museum of the Year; Datong City Library (China, 2008–13); and the Taiyuan Museum of Art (Taiyuan, China, 2009–13, see p. 324). Current works

include the Taubman College of Architecture and Urban Planning expansion, University of Michigan (Ann Arbor, Michigan, USA, 2014–16); and the Cape Rep Theater expansion (Brewster, Massachusetts, USA, 2014–16).

COOP HIMMELB(L)AU → p.108

Coop Himmelb(l)au
Wolf D. Prix & Partner ZT GmbH
Spengergasse 37
1050 Vienna, Austria

Tel: +43 1 54 66 00
Fax: +43 1 54 66 06 00
E-mail: office@coop-himmelblau.at
Web: www.coop-himmelblau.at

Coop Himmelb(l)au was founded by Wolf D. Prix, Helmut Swiczinsky, and Michael Holzer in Vienna, Austria, in 1968. In 1988, a second studio was opened in Los Angeles, USA. Today the studio is directed by Wolf D. Prix, Harald Krieger, Karolin Schmidbaur, Louise Kiesling, and Project Partners. WOLF D. PRIX was born in 1942 in Vienna, and educated at the Technical University, Vienna, at SCI-Arc, and at the Architectural Association (AA), London. From 1993 to 2011 he was Professor of Architecture at the University of Applied Arts in Vienna, where he also served as Vice-Rector from 2003 to 2012, and he has headed Studio Prix since 2003. Completed projects of the group include the East Pavilion of the Groninger Museum (Groningen, the Netherlands, 1990–94); the UFA Cinema Center (Dresden, Germany, 1993–98); the Academy of Fine Arts (Munich, Germany, 1992/2002–05); Akron Art Museum (Akron, Ohio, USA, 2001–07); BMW Welt (Munich, Germany, 2001–07); Central Los Angeles Area High School #9 for the Visual and Performing Arts (Los Angeles, California, USA, 2002–08); Busan Cinema Center (Busan, South Korea, 2005–11); Martin Luther Church (Hainburg, Austria, 2008–11); Dalian International Conference Center (Dalian, China, 2008–12, see p. 108); Musée des Confluences (Lyon, France, 2001–14); European Central Bank (Frankfurt, Germany, 2003–14); and the House of Music (Aalborg, Denmark, 2008–14).

JAVIER CORVALÁN → pp.62, 346

Javier Corvalán + Laboratorio de Arquitectura, Ramos Alfaro 299
Luque, Paraguay

Tel/Fax: +595 2164 6777
E-mail: arq.javiercorvalan@gmail.com
Web: www.laboratoriodearquitectura.com.py

JAVIER CORVALÁN ESPINOLA was born in Asunción, Paraguay, in 1962. He obtained his degree as an architect from the Faculty of Science and Technology of the UCA (Universidad Católica Nuestra Señora de la Asunción, 1981–87). He created his own studio in 1990. He is Visiting Professor at the IUAV University in Venice (Italy). His work includes the Sotoportego House (2009); Hamaca House (2009, see p. 62), the Subeldía House (2010); the APG Public Golf Driving Range (2013, see p. 346); and the Sports Center of the Paraguayan Olympic Committee (2014–), all in the area of Luque, Paraguay.

ENTRESITIO → p.70

estudio.entresitio
Gran Vía 33, 7º
28013 Madrid
Spain

Tel: +34 917 01 03 30
Fax: +34 917 01 03 31
E-mail: estudio@entresitio.com
Web: www.entresitio.com

The Principals of the firm are MARÍA HURTADO DE MENDOZA WAHROLEN, born in Madrid in 1968 (ETSAM, 1993), CÉSAR JIMÉNEZ DE TEJADA BENAVIDES, born in Madrid in 1964 (ETSAM 1992, MS AAD 2000 / CUNY), and JOSÉ MARÍA HURTADO DE MENDOZA WAHROLÉN, born in Madrid in 1973 (ETSAM 1999). The first two worked together beginning in 1993 and were joined by José María Hurtado in 2004 after a period in the office of Rafael Moneo. Their built work includes a public diagnostic and treatment center (Daimiel, 2007); the Tower (Madrid, 2009); and the trilogy of healthcare centers San Blas+Usera+Villaverde (Madrid 2005–10), all in Spain. More recently they completed #House#1 (Madrid, 2011–13, see p. 70). Their body of work also includes a large number of interesting competition entries.

HÉCTOR FERNÁNDEZ ELORZA
→ pp.394, 412

Héctor Fernández Elorza
Avenida de Bruselas 75, bajo
28028 Madrid, Spain

Tel: +34 696 99 66 14
E-mail: helorza@yahoo.com
Web: www.hfelorza.com

HÉCTOR FERNÁNDEZ ELORZA was born in Zaragoza, Spain, in 1972. He was awarded a scholarship from the EU-exchange program at the Darmstadt Institute of Technology (1995–96) and at the Royal Technical Institute of Stockholm (1997–98). He received his degree in Architecture at the ETSAM in 1998. He did postgraduate studies in Scandinavia, with a grant from the Marghit and Folke Perzhon Foundation (1999–2000). This period was dedicated to research at the Architectural Museum Archive in Stockholm and the Alvar Aalto Foundation in Helsinki. He has been a Professor at the ETSAM since 2001. His work includes an exhibition center and lecture hall for the Nuevos Ministerios (Madrid, 2003–06); the Zoology Department, University of Alcalá—UAH (Alcalá de Henares, 2004–07); a laboratory building, University of Alcalá—UAH (Alcalá de Henares, 2004–09); an architecture studio (Madrid, 2007–10); Venecia Park (Zaragoza, 2009–12, see p. 394); and the Faculty of Cellular and Genetic Biology, University of Alcalá—UAH (Alcalá de Henares, 2009–12, see p. 412), all in Spain.

ANDREAS FUHRIMANN GABRIELLE HÄCHLER → pp.28, 380

Andreas Fuhrimann Gabrielle Hächler Architekten, Hardturm Str. 66
8005 Zurich, Switzerland

Tel: +41 44 271 04 80
E-mail: mail@afgh.ch
Web: www.afgh.ch

ANDREAS FUHRIMANN was born in 1956 in Zurich, Switzerland. He studied physics and architecture at the ETH Zurich and obtained his degree in Architecture there in 1985. In 1988, he was a lecturer at the School of Design and Crafts in "interior architecture." He has worked with Gabrielle Hächler since 1995. GABRIELLE HÄCHLER was born in 1958 in Aarau, Switzerland. She studied Art History at Zurich University, and architecture at the ETH Zurich, where she obtained her degree in 1988. As of 1988, she had her own architectural office and held an assistant lecturer's position in the Department of Construction at the ETH. Their work includes an apartment building at

Uetliberg (Zurich, 2003); Eva Presenhuber House in Vnà (Engadine, 2007); a cemetery building (Erlenbach, Lake Zurich, 2010); an apartment building on Röntgenstrasse (Zurich, 2010); an artist's house (Würenlos, 2010–12, see p. 28); and the Rotsee Finish Tower (Lucerne, 2012–13, see p. 380), all in Switzerland.

SOU FUJIMOTO → pp.132, 306

Sou Fujimoto Architects
6F Ichikawa Seihon Building
10–3 Higashienoki, Shinjuku
Tokyo 162–0807, Japan

Tel: +81 3 3513 5401
Fax: +81 3 3513 5402
E-mail: media@sou-fujimoto.net
Web: www.sou-fujimoto.net

SOU FUJIMOTO was born in 1971. He received a B.Arch degree from the University of Tokyo, Faculty of Engineering, Department of Architecture (1990–94). He established his own firm, Sou Fujimoto Architects, in 2000. He is considered one of the most interesting rising Japanese architects, and his forms usually evade easy classification. His work includes the Industrial Training Facilities for the Mentally Handicapped (Hokkaido, 2003); Environment Art Forum, Annaka (Gunma, 2003–06); Treatment Center for Mentally Disturbed Children (Hokkaido, 2006); House O (Chiba, 2007); N House (Oita Prefecture, 2007–08); and the Final Wooden House (Kumamura, Kumamoto, 2007–08). Other recent work includes the Musashino Art University Museum and Library (Tokyo, 2007–09); House H (Tokyo, 2008–09); Tokyo Apartment (Itabashiku, Tokyo, 2009–10); the Uniqlo Store in Shinsaibashi (Osaka, 2010); House NA (Tokyo, 2010); House K (Nishinomiya-shi, Hyogo, 2011–12); a public toilet (Ichihara, Chiba, 2012, see p. 132); and the Serpentine Gallery Summer Pavilion (Kensington Gardens, London, UK, 2013, see p. 306), all in Japan unless stated otherwise. He received the Golden Lion (Best National Participation) for his design of the Japanese Pavilion exhibition (Architecture Biennale, Venice, Italy, 2012).

MASSIMILIANO AND DORIANA FUKSAS → pp.150, 292

Massimiliano and Doriana Fuksas
Piazza del Monte di Pietà 30
00186 Rome, Italy

Tel: +39 06 68 80 78 71
Fax: +39 06 68 80 78 72
E-mail: press@fuksas.com
Web: www.fuksas.com

MASSIMILIANO FUKSAS was born in 1944 in Rome, Italy. He received his degree in Architecture at the "La Sapienza" University of Rome in 1969. He founded a studio in Rome in 1967, and opened an office in Paris in 1989. He won the 1999 Grand Prix d'Architecture in France. He was the Director of the 7th Architecture Biennale in Venice (1998–2000). He has worked with DORIANA MANDRELLI FUKSAS since 1985. She attended the Faculty of Architecture at the "La Sapienza" University of Rome and has been responsible for design in the firm since 1997. They have completed the Ferrari Operational Headquarters and Research Center (Maranello, Italy, 2001–04); the new Trade Fair (Rho-Pero, Milan, Italy, 2002–05); Zenith Strasbourg (Eckbolsheim, Strasbourg, France, 2003–07); the Armani Ginza Tower (Tokyo, Japan, 2005–07); Peres Peace House (Jaffa, Israel, 1999–2009); Emporio Armani Fifth Avenue (New York, New York, USA, 2007–09); MyZeil Shopping Mall (Frankfurt, Germany, 2009); and the Admirant Entrance Building (Eindhoven, the Netherlands, 2003–10). Recent work includes the House of Justice (Tblisi, Georgia, 2010–12); the Georges-Frêche School of Hotel Management (Montpellier, France 2010–12); the New National Archives of France (Paris, France, 2009–13, see p. 292); and Terminal 3, International Shenzhen Bao'an Airport (Shenzhen, China, 2010–13, see p. 150). They are currently working on the Guosen Securities Tower (Shenzhen, China, 2010–); the CBD Cultural Center (Beijing, China, 2013–); and have won the competions for the renovation of Beverly Center (Los Angeles, California, USA, 2012); and the Moscow Polytechnic Museum and Educational Center (Moscow, Russia, 2013).

ZAIGA GAILE → p.338

Zaigas Gailes Birojs
Marijas iela 13/IV, Riga 1050, Latvia

Tel: +371 67 81 20 88
Fax: +371 67 81 20 89
E-mail: zgb@zgb.lv, Web: www.zgb.lv

ZAIGA GAILE was born in 1951 in Riga, Latvia. She graduated from Riga

Technical University with a degree in Architecture in 1975 and founded her own firm in 1992. Her work and professional interests focus on renovation and reconstruction projects. The most significant of these, some of which are still ongoing, are the Bergs Bazaar, the first historic retail arcade in Riga (1993–); the renovation of 10 19th-century houses (Ķīpsala, Riga, 1997–); the conversion of a Soviet-era fish-farm pumping station into a family vacation home (Kaltene, Talsi district, 2006–10); the conversion of a gypsum factory into a residential complex with a restaurant and a yacht pier (Ķīpsala, Riga, 2004–13); and the reconstruction of the Rumene Manor (Kandava district, 2005–), all in Latvia. The Žanis Lipke Memorial in Ķīpsala (Riga, 2008–12, see p. 338) is one of her few new architecture designs.

FRANK O. GEHRY → p.252

Gehry Partners, LLP
12541 Beatrice Street
Los Angeles, CA 90066, USA

Tel: +1 310 482 3000
E-mail: info@foga.com
Web: www.foga.com

Born in Toronto, Canada, in 1929, FRANK GEHRY studied at the University of Southern California, Los Angeles (1949–51), and at Harvard (1956–57). Principal of Frank O. Gehry and Associates, Inc., Los Angeles, since 1962, he received the Pritzker Prize in 1989, the Praemium Imperiale in 1992, and the Prince of Asturias Prize in 2014. His early work in California included the redesign of his own house, and the construction of a number of other houses, such as the Norton Residence (Venice, 1984) and the Schnabel Residence (Brentwood, 1989). His first foreign projects included Festival Disney (Marne-la-Vallée, France, 1989–92); and the Guggenheim Bilbao (Spain, 1991–97), which is felt by some to be one of the most significant buildings of the late 20th century. Other work includes the DG Bank Headquarters (Berlin, Germany, 2001); the Fisher Center for the Performing Arts at Bard College (Annandale-on-Hudson, New York, USA, 2003); and the Walt Disney Concert Hall (Los Angeles, USA, 2003). More recent work includes a Maggie's Center (Dundee, Scotland, 1999–2003); the Jay Pritzker Pavilion in Millennium Park (Chicago, USA, 2004); the Hotel at

the Marques de Riscal winery (Elciego, Spain, 2003–07); his first New York building, the InterActiveCorp Headquarters (New York, USA, 2003–07); an extension of the Art Gallery of Ontario (Toronto, Canada, 2005–08); and, again in New York, the Eight Spruce Street Tower (New York, USA, 2007–11). He recently completed the Biodiversity Museum (Panama City, Panama, 2004–14); the Louis Vuitton Foundation in the Bois de Boulogne in Paris (France, 2008–14, see p. 252); and the Dr Chau Chak Wing Building (Sydney, Australia, 2012–14).

SEAN GODSELL → p.440

Sean Godsell Architects
2/49 Exhibition Street
Melbourne, VIC 3000, Australia

Tel: +61 3 9654 2677
Fax: +61 3 9654 3877
E-mail: info@seangodsell.com
Web: www.seangodsell.com

SEAN GODSELL was born in Melbourne, Australia, in 1960. He graduated from the University of Melbourne in 1984 and worked from 1986 to 1988 in London with Sir Denys Lasdun. He created Godsell Associates Pty Ltd. Architects in 1994. After receiving an M.Arch degree from RMIT University (Melbourne, 1999), he was a finalist in the Seppelt Contemporary Art Awards held by the Museum of Contemporary Art in Sydney for his work "Future Shack." He won the RAIA Award of Merit for new residential work for the Carter/Tucker House in 2000 (Breamlea, Victoria, 1999–2000). His work also includes Peninsula House (Victoria, 2001–02); Woodleigh School Science Faculty (Baxter, Victoria, 2002); Lewis House (Dunkeld, Victoria, 2003); Westwood House (Sydney, 2003); ACN Headquarters (Victoria, 2003); and St. Andrews Beach House (Mornington Peninsula, Victoria, 2003–05). Recent work includes Edward Street House (Melbourne, 2008–11); Kew Studio (Kew, Victoria, 2009–11); Tanderra House (Victoria, 2005–12); and the RMIT Design Hub (Melbourne, 2007–12, see p. 440), all in Australia.

ZAHA HADID → p.216

Zaha Hadid Architects, Studio 9
10 Bowling Green Lane
London EC1R 0BQ, UK

Tel: +44 20 72 53 51 47
Fax: +44 20 72 51 83 22
E-mail: press@zaha-hadid.com
Web: www.zaha-hadid.com

ZAHA HADID studied architecture at the Architectural Association (AA) in London, beginning in 1972, and was awarded the Diploma Prize in 1977. She then became a Partner of Rem Koolhaas in OMA and taught at the AA. She has also taught at Harvard, the University of Chicago, in Hamburg, and at Columbia University in New York. In 2004, Zaha Hadid became the first woman to win the coveted Pritzker Prize. She completed the Vitra Fire Station (Weil am Rhein, Germany, 1990–94); and exhibition designs such as that for "The Great Utopia" (Solomon R. Guggenheim Museum, New York, USA, 1992). More recently, Zaha Hadid has entered a phase of active construction with such projects as the Lois & Richard Rosenthal Center for Contemporary Art (Cincinnati, Ohio, USA, 1999–2003); Phaeno Science Center (Wolfsburg, Germany, 2001–05); Ordrupgaard Museum Extension (Copenhagen, Denmark, 2001–05); the Central Building of the new BMW Assembly Plant in Leipzig (Germany, 2005); the Mobile Art, Chanel Contemporary Art Container (various locations, 2007–); and the MAXXI, the National Museum of 21st Century Arts (Rome, Italy, 1998–2009). Recent projects include the Sheikh Zayed Bridge (Abu Dhabi, UAE, 2003–10); the Guangzhou Opera House (Guangzhou, China, 2005–10); the Aquatics Center for the London 2012 Olympic Games (London, UK, 2005–11); the CMA CGM Tower (Marseille, France, 2008–11); Pierresvives (Montpellier, France, 2002–12); the Heydar Aliyev Center (Baku, Azerbaijan, 2007–12, see p. 216); and "Arum" at the Corderie dell'Arsenale (Venice, Italy, 2012).

HENEGHAN PENG → p.210

Heneghan Peng Architects
14–16 Lord Edward Street
Dublin 2, Ireland

Tel: +353 1 633 90 00
Fax: +353 1 633 90 10
E-mail: hparc@hparc.com
Web: www.hparc.com

Heneghan Peng Architects was founded in New York in 1999 by Róisín Heneghan and Shih-Fu Peng. The firm moved to Dublin, Ireland, in 2001. With a staff of just four people, the firm won the international competition to design the Grand Egyptian Museum in 2003 over 1557 other entries. RÓISÍN HENEGHAN obtained her B.Arch degree from University College Dublin (1987) and her M.Arch from the Harvard GSD (1992). SHIH-FU PENG received his B.Arch from Cornell (1989) and his M.Arch from Harvard in 1992. Their projects include Áras Chill Dara, Local Government Offices (Kildare, Ireland, 2001–05); Central Park Bridges and Landscaping, London 2012 Olympic Park (London, UK, 2007–10); and the Giant's Causeway Visitor Center (County Antrim, UK, 2010–12, see p. 210). Ongoing projects under construction include the Grand Egyptian Museum—Museum, Conservation Center, and Conference Center (Giza, Cairo, Egypt, 2004–15); the National Gallery of Ireland Extension and Refurbishment (Dublin, Ireland, 2007–15); and the Arabsat Headquarters building (Riyadh, Saudi Arabia, 2008–15). At the end of 2013, they won an international competition to design the National Center for Contemporary Arts (NCCA) at Khodynskoye Pole in Moscow, Russia.

HERZOG & DE MEURON

→ pp. 298, 398

Herzog & de Meuron
Rheinschanze 6
4056 Basel, Switzerland

Tel: +41 61 385 57 57
Fax: +41 61 385 57 58
E-mail: info@herzogdemeuron.com
Web: www.herzogdemeuron.com

JACQUES HERZOG and PIERRE DE MEURON were both born in Basel, Switzerland, in 1950. They received degrees in Architecture from the ETH Zurich in 1975, after studying with Aldo Rossi, and founded their partnership in Basel in 1978. The partnership has grown over the years: CHRISTINE BINSWANGER joined the practice as Partner in 1994, successively followed by ASCAN MERGENTHALER in 2004 and STEFAN MARBACH in 2006. Herzog & de Meuron won the 2001 Pritzker Prize, and both the RIBA Gold Medal and Praemium Imperiale in 2007. Many of their projects are public facilities, such as Tate Modern in London (UK, 1998–2000), and its extension the Tate Modern Project (2005–2016); and the National Stadium, the Main Stadium for the 2008 Olympic Games in Beijing

(China, 2004–08). Among their latest works are the new Parrish Art Museum in Water Mill (New York, USA, 2010–12); Volkshaus Basel, Bar, Brasserie (Basel, Switzerland, 2011–12, see p. 398); the New Hall for Messe Basel (Basel, Switzerland, 2010–13); the Pérez Art Museum Miami (Miami, Florida, USA, 2010–13, see p. 298); the Arena do Morro at Mãe Luiza (Natal, Brazil, 2012–14); and the Ricola Kräuterzentrum (Laufen, Switzerland, 2014). Projects currently under construction include Nouveau Stade de Bordeaux (Bordeaux, France, 2015); the Elbphilharmonie Hamburg (Hamburg, Germany, 2016); and the Porta Volta Fondazione Feltrinelli (Milan, Italy, 2016).

JAKOB + MACFARLANE → p. 246

Jakob + MacFarlane sarl d'Architecture
13 Rue des Petites Écuries
75010 Paris, France

Tel: +33 1 44 79 05 72
Fax: +33 1 48 00 97 93
E-mail: info@jakobmacfarlane.com
Web: www.jakobmacfarlane.com

DOMINIQUE JAKOB was born in 1966 and holds a degree in Art History from the Université de Paris I (1990) and a degree in Architecture from the École d'Architecture Paris-Villemin (1991). Born in New Zealand in 1961, BRENDAN MACFARLANE received his B.Arch at SCI-Arc (1984), and his M.Arch degree at the Harvard GSD (1990). From 1995 to 1997, MacFarlane was an architecture critic at the Architectural Association (AA) in London. They founded their own agency in 1992 in Paris, and were also cofounders with E. Marin-Trottin and D. Trottin of the exhibition and conference organizer Periphériques (1996–98). Their main projects include the Georges Restaurant (Pompidou Center, Paris, 1999–2000); the restructuring of the Maxime Gorki Theater (Petit-Quevilly, 1999–2000); and the Renault International Communication Center (Boulogne, 2004). Recent and current work includes the City of Fashion and Design (Paris, 2007–08); another dock project, the Orange Cube (Lyon, 2010); Wanderlust (Paris, 2012); Les Turbulences, the FRAC Contemporary Art and Architecture Center in Orléans (2010–13, see p. 246); Green Pavilion, Lyon Confluence, Euronews Headquarters (Lyon, 2013); Maison S (Boulogne-Billancourt, 2014); Gaumont Parnasse Cinema (Paris, 2015); and Boerenboom

Square (Knokke-Heist, Belgium, 2015), all in France unless stated otherwise.

ANISH KAPOOR AND ARATA ISOZAKI

→ p. 264

Anish Kapoor Studio
London, UK

E-mail: info@kapoorstudio.com
Web: www.anishkapoor.com

Isozaki, Aoki & Associates Co., Ltd.
6–13–13 Akasaka, Minato-Ku
Tokyo 107-0052
Japan

Tel: +81 3 3405 5505
Fax: +81 3 3505 4747
E-mail: info@i-a-a.co.jp
Web: www.i-a-a.co.jp

The artist ANISH KAPOOR was born in Bombay, India, in 1954 and has lived and worked in London since the early 1970s. He studied at the Hornsey College of Art (1973–77) and the Chelsea School of Art (1977–78), and he had his first solo exhibition in 1980. He represented Britain at the 1990 Biennale in Venice and won the Turner Prize in 1991. His many exhibitions include architectural scale works such as "Marsyas" (Tate Modern, London, UK, October 2002–April 2003); and "Leviathan," Monumenta 2011 (Grand Palais, Paris, France, 11 May–23 June, 2011). Permanent public works include "Cloud Gate," Chicago Millennium Park (Chicago, Illinois, USA, 2004); "Temenos" (Middlehaven Dock, Middlesbrough, UK, 2004); and "Orbit" (Olympic Park, London, UK, 2012).

Born in Oita City on the Island of Kyushu, Japan, in 1931, ARATA ISOZAKI graduated from the Architectural Faculty of the University of Tokyo in 1954, worked with Kenzo Tange, and then established Arata Isozaki & Associates in 1963. Winner of the 1986 RIBA Gold Medal, his notable early buildings include the Museum of Contemporary Art (Los Angeles, California, USA, 1981–86); Art Tower Mito (Ibaraki, Japan, 1986–90); and the Center of Science and Industry (COSI, Columbus, Ohio, USA, 1994–99). More recent work includes the Shenzhen Cultural Center (Shenzhen, China, 1998–2008); Central Academy of Fine Art, Museum of Art (Beijing, China, 2003–08); Himalayas Center (Shanghai, China, 2003–11); Qatar National Convention Center (Doha,

Qatar, 2004–11]; and the ongoing Zhengdong New District Long Hu Area, Sub CDB, Master Plan [Zhengzhou, China, 2010–]. HIROSHI AOKI was born in 1952 in Tokyo. A Director of Arata Isozaki & Associates beginning in 1975, he became Representative Director of the reorganized firm Isozaki, Aoki & Associates in 2011. Together with the artist Anish Kapoor, the firm realized the Lucerne Festival ARK NOVA [Matsushima, Miyagi, Japan, 2013] published here, see p. 264.

KARRES EN BRANDS → p.200

Karres en Brands landscape architecture + urban planning
Oude Amersfoortseweg 123
1212 AA Hilversum, The Netherlands

Tel: +31 35 642 29 62
E-mail: info@karresenbrands.nl
Web: www.karresenbrands.nl

SYLVIA KARRES, born in 1956, studied landscape architecture at the State College of Gardening and Landscaping in Boskoop and at the Academy of Architecture in Amsterdam. She worked at Bureau Maas, as well as for the Province of North Holland, and for 10 years as a designer and project manager at Bureau Bakker and Bleeker (now B+B) in Amsterdam. In 1997, she founded Karres en Brands Landscape Architecture with Bart Brands. She is Director and co-owner of Karres en Brands. BART BRANDS was born in 1962 and also studied landscape architecture at the State College of Gardening and Landscaping in Boskoop and urbanism at the Academy of Architecture in Amsterdam. After working for the municipality of The Hague, he worked at Bureau Bakker and Bleeker (1991–97), before cofounding Karres en Brands. He is also Director and co-owner of the firm. Their work includes Ecomare [Texel, 2012]; the Trompenburg park ['s-Graveland, 2012]; the landscaping of the Statens Museum for Kunst [Copenhagen, Denmark, 2014]; Nieuwe Ooster Cemetery [Amsterdam, 2005–, see p. 200]; and Bosrijk [Eindhoven, 2008–], all in the Netherlands unless stated otherwise.

KENGO KUMA → pp.206, 408

KAE [Kuma Associates Europe]
16 Rue Martel, 75010 Paris, France

Tel: +33 1 44 88 94 90
Fax: +33 9 56 88 94 90
E-mail: kuma@kkaa.eu
Web: www.kkaa.co.jp

Born in 1954 in Kanagawa, Japan, KENGO KUMA graduated in 1979 from the University of Tokyo with an M.Arch degree. In 1987, he established the Spatial Design Studio, and in 1991 he created Kengo Kuma & Associates. His recent work includes the Great [Bamboo] Wall Guesthouse [Beijing, China, 2002]; One Omotesando [Tokyo, 2003]; LVMH Osaka [Osaka, 2004]; the Nagasaki Prefectural Art Museum [Nagasaki, 2005]; Zhongtai Box, Z58 building [Shanghai, China, 2003–06]; Steel House [Bunkyo-ku, Tokyo, 2005–07]; Tiffany Ginza [Tokyo, 2008]; Nezu Museum [Tokyo, 2007–09]; Museum of Kanayama [Ota City, Gunma, 2009]; Glass Wood House [New Canaan, Connecticut, USA, 2007–10]; Yusuhara Marche [Yusuhara, Kochi, 2009–10]; and the Yusuhara Wooden Bridge Museum [Yusuhara-cho, Takaoka-gun, Kochi, 2010], all in Japan unless stated otherwise. Two recent small projects [Même Experimental House, Hokkaido, 2011–12; and Hojo-an [Kyoto, 2012] demonstrate the architect's attachment to innovative structures, often based on historic precedents. As the two projects published here attest, the architect has also begun to work extensively in Europe: FRAC PACA [Marseille, France, 2011–13, see p. 206]; and the Conservatory of Music, Dance, and Theater [Aix-en-Provence, France, 2011–13, see p. 408].

YAYOI KUSAMA → p.226

David Zwirner
519, 525 & 533 West 19th Street
New York, NY 10011, USA

Tel: +1 212 727 2070
Fax: +1 212 727 2072
E-mail: information@davidzwirner.com
Web: www.davidzwirner.com

The artist YAYOI KUSAMA was born in 1929 in Matsumoto, Japan. She attended the Kyoto Municipal School of Arts and Crafts [Kyoto, 1948–49], and today lives and works in Tokyo. Since her first solo show in Japan in 1952, Yayoi Kusama's work has been featured widely in both solo and group presentations. Her most recent solo museum exhibition in New York was at the Whitney Museum of American Art in 2012. Organized by Tate Modern, London, it was previously shown at the Museo Nacional Centro de Arte Reina Sofía, Madrid, and the Centre Georges Pompidou, Paris. Other museums that have hosted recent solo exhibitions of the artist's work include Malba—Fundación Costantini, Buenos Aires; Daegu Art Museum, South Korea [both 2013]; and Museo Tamayo Arte Contemporáneo, Mexico City [2014]. Considered to be a precursor of both Pop and Minimalist art, the artist's work spans a broad variety of mediums that include painting, sculpture, performance, installation, and design, which share an interest in repetition, pattern, and bright "psychedelic" colors. Yayoi Kusama is represented by David Zwirner in New York, Victoria Miro in London, and Ota Fine Arts in Tokyo and Singapore. See page 226 for the two works published here.

MBA/S → p.66

MBA/S Matthias Bauer Associates
Rotebühlstr. 44, 70178 Stuttgart
Germany

Tel: +49 711 24 89 33 0
E-mail: office@mbas.de
Web: www.mbas.de

MATTHIAS BAUER was born in Stuttgart, Germany, in 1962. He received a degree in Architecture and Urban Planning from the University of Stuttgart in 1992. He worked in the office of OMA/Rem Koolhaas [Rotterdam, 1993] and at Brunet & Saunier Architectes [Paris, 1994–95], before becoming a Project Partner at OMA/Rem Koolhaas [Rotterdam 1995–98]. He founded MBA/S in Rotterdam in 1997. The firm has been based in Stuttgart since 1999. His recent work includes a skatepark [Stuttgart, 2008]; the Dior Flagship Store in Geneva [Switzerland, 2013]; the UN Campus [Bonn, 2013]; the Art Park [Baltic Sea, 2013]; and House 36 [Stuttgart, 2012–14, see p. 66], all in Germany unless otherwise stated.

MECANOO → p.360

Mecanoo architecten
Oude Delft 203
2611 HD Delft, The Netherlands

Tel: +31 15 279 81 00
E-mail: info@mecanoo.nl
Web: www.mecanoo.nl

Mecanoo was founded while FRANCINE HOUBEN, Creative Director, and two others were still studying, forming the company in 1984. Today the team numbers more than 120, and includes AART FRANSEN as Technical Director, PETER HAASBROEK as Financial Director, and Partners DICK VAN GAMEREN, PAUL KETELAAR, FRANCESCO VEENSTRA, and ELLEN VAN DER WAL. Main works include the Delft University of Technology Library [Delft, the Netherlands, 1996–98]; St. Mary of the Angels Chapel in the St. Lawrence Cemetery [Rotterdam, the Netherlands, 2000–01]; the La Llotja Theater and Congress Center in Lleida [Spain, 2006–10]; Kaap Skil, Maritime and Beachcombers Museum [Oudeschild, Texel, the Netherlands, 2010–11]; the Bruce C. Bolling Municipal Building [Boston, Massachusetts, USA, 2012–14]; and the Library of Birmingham integrated with the REP Theater [Birmingham, UK, 2010–13, see p. 360]. Ongoing work includes the Delft Municipal Offices and Train Station [Delft, the Netherlands, 2012–16]; and Wei Wu Ying Center for the Performing Arts [Kaohsiung, Taiwan, 2010–16].

RICHARD MEIER → p.164

Richard Meier & Partners
Architects LLP,
1001 Gayley Avenue
Los Angeles, CA 90024, USA

Tel: +1 310 208 6464
Fax: +1 310 824 2294
E-mail: mail@richardmeier.com
Web: www.richardmeier.com

RICHARD MEIER was born in Newark, New Jersey, in 1934. He received his architectural training at Cornell University, and worked in the office of Marcel Breuer (1960–63), before establishing his own practice in 1963. In 1984, he became the youngest winner of the Pritzker Prize, and he received the 1988 RIBA Gold Medal. His notable buildings include the Atheneum [New Harmony, Indiana, USA, 1975–79]; High Museum of Art [Atlanta, Georgia, USA, 1980–83]; Museum of Decorative Arts [Frankfurt, Germany, 1979–84]; Canal+ Headquarters [Paris, France, 1988–91]; Barcelona Museum of Contemporary Art [Barcelona, Spain, 1988–95]; City Hall and Library [The Hague, the Netherlands, 1990–95]; and the Getty Center [Los Angeles, California, USA, 1984–97]. Recent work includes the United States Courthouse and Federal Building [Phoenix, Arizona, USA, 1995–2000]; Jubilee Church [Rome, Italy, 1996–2003]; Ara Pacis Museum [Rome, Italy, 1995–2006]; 165 Charles Street [New York, New York, USA, 2003–06]; and the Arp Museum [Rolandseck, Germany, 1997–2007]. More recently he has completed the ECM City Tower [Pankrác, Prague, Czech Republic, 2001–08]; Italcementi i.lab [Bergamo, Italy, 2008–12]; OCT Shenzhen Clubhouse [Shenzhen, China, 2010–12]; the United States Courthouse [San Diego, California, 2003–13, see p. 164]; the Rothschild Tower [Tel Aviv, Israel, 2007–15]; and the Leblon Offices [Rio de Janeiro, Brazil, 2011–15].

MTM → pp.404, 436

MTM Arquitectos, Clavel 5, 1°B
28004 Madrid, Spain

Tel: +34 91 523 77 68
Fax: +34 91 523 73 86
E-mail: mtm@mtmarquitectos.com
Web: www.mtmarquitectos.com

JAVIER FRESNEDA was born in 1965 and JAVIER SANJUÁN in 1964. They founded MTM Arquitectos, and have worked as associates since 1997. Both graduated as architects from the ETSAM in Madrid [Spain, 1991]. They worked in the office of Abalos & Herreros from 1990 to 1993. Javier Sanjuán also worked with 3AC in 1994. To date, MTM has carried forward a total of 28 projects, of which 17 have been built. Their work includes 22 social-housing units [Avilés, Asturias, 2002–04]; an extension of the Pharmacy School of the University of Madrid [Complutense, 2001–06]; La Cañada Civic Center [Torrejón, Madrid, 2003–06]; Pormetxeta Square [Barakaldo, Bizcaya, 2006–10]; the Plaza Mayor Services Building, UAM [Cantoblanco Campus, Madrid, 2009–12, see p. 436]; and the Center for Biomedical Research of Aragon [CIBA] [Zaragoza, 2008–13, see p. 404], all in Spain.

RYUE NISHIZAWA → p.124

Office of Ryue Nishizawa
1-5-27 Tatsumi, Koto
Tokyo 135-0053, Japan

Tel: +81 3 5534 0117
Fax: +81 3 5534 1757
E-mail: office@ryuenishizawa.com
Web: www.ryuenishizawa.com

RYUE NISHIZAWA was born in Tokyo in 1966. He graduated from Yokohama National University with an M.Arch in 1990, and joined the office of Kazuyo Sejima & Associates in Tokyo the same year. In 1995, he established SANAA with Kazuyo Sejima, and two years later his own practice, the Office of Ryue Nishizawa. He has worked on all the significant projects of SANAA and has been a Visiting Professor at Yokohama National University [2001–], the University of Singapore [2003], Princeton [2006], and the Harvard GSD [2007]. His work outside SANAA includes a Weekend House [Gunma, 1998]; the N Museum [Kagawa, 2005]; Moriyama House [Tokyo, 2006]; House A [East Japan, 2006]; Towada Art Center [Aomori, 2006–08]; the Teshima Museum [Teshima, Kagawa, 2009–10]; a garden and house [Tokyo, 2010–11]; the Hiroshi Senju Museum [Karuizawa, Nagano, 2011]; and Fukita Pavilion in Shodoshima [Shodoshima, Kagawa, 2013, see p. 124], all in Japan.

NLÉ → p.430

NLÉ, Brouwersgracht 821
1015 GK Amsterdam, The Netherlands

E-mail: contact@nleworks.com
Web: www.nleworks.com

KUNLÉ ADEYEMI is an architect, urbanist, and designer. He is at present best known for creating the Makoko Floating School [see p. 430]. This project is part of an extensive research effort called "African Water Cities" being developed by NLÉ, a practice founded by Adeyemi in 2010, with a focus on developing cities and communities. Born in 1976 and raised in Kaduna, Nigeria, Adeyemi studied architecture at the University of Lagos, where he began his early practice, before joining OMA in 2002. Here he led the design, development, and execution of several large prestigious projects in Europe, Asia, Africa, and the Middle East, including the Shenzhen Stock Exchange tower in China [see p. 136], the Qatar National Library in Doha, and Prada Transformer in Seoul. The work of NLÉ includes the Nike Art Pavilion [Lagos, 2011]; Yaba Prototype [Lagos, 2011]; Mabushi Residential Development [Abuja, 2012]; Makoko Floating School [Lagos, 2012–13, see p. 430]; Chicoco Radio [Port Harcourt, 2013]; and the Bloomsbury Waterfront Office Building [Lagos, 2013], all in Nigeria.

NO ARCHITECTURE → p. 38

NO ARCHITECTURE, PLLC
176 Elizabeth Street 2A
New York, NY 10012, USA

Tel: +1 646 662 9881
E-mail: info@noarchitecture.com
Web: www.noarchitecture.com

ANDREW HEID is the founding Principal of NO Architecture (NOA). Born in Eugene, Oregon, in 1980, he received a B.A. degree from Yale University (2002), before working in the offices of David Adjaye in London and Robert A. M. Stern in New York (2002–03). He received his M.Arch degree from Princeton University in 2006. From 2005 to 2008, he worked with REX and OMA in New York and Rotterdam, and then founded NO Architecture in New York in 2009. NOA has participated in numerous international competitions in Germany, Switzerland, Taiwan, and Korea. NOA has recently completed the Courtyard House (Aurora, Oregon, 2012–13, see p. 38); while ongoing work includes the Allegheny Mountain House (Deep Creek Lake, Maryland, 2010–); and 75 First Avenue, a luxury condominium building in New York (New York, 2012–), all in the USA.

JEAN NOUVEL → pp. 118, 374

Ateliers Jean Nouvel
10 Cité d'Angoulême
75011 Paris, France

Tel: +33 1 49 23 83 83
Fax: +33 1 43 14 81 10
E-mail: info@jeannouvel.fr
Web: www.jeannouvel.com

JEAN NOUVEL was born in 1945 in Fumel, France. He studied in Bordeaux and then at the École des Beaux-Arts (Paris, 1964–72). From 1967 to 1970, he was an assistant of the noted architects Claude Parent and Paul Virilio. He created his first office with François Seigneur in Paris in 1970. Jean Nouvel received the RIBA Gold Medal in 2001 and the Pritzker Prize in 2008. His first widely noted project was the Institut du Monde Arabe (Paris, France, 1981–87, with Architecture Studio) and the Fondation Cartier (Paris, France, 1991–94) made him one of the most noted French architects. Major projects since 2000 are the Music and Conference Center (Lucerne, Switzerland, 1998–2000); Agbar Tower (Barcelona,

Spain, 1999–2005); an extension of the Reina Sofia Museum (Madrid, Spain, 1999–2005); the Quai Branly Museum (Paris, France, 1999–2006); the Guthrie Theater (Minneapolis, Minnesota, USA, 2001–06); "40 Mercer" apartment building in SoHo (New York, New York, USA, 2005–08); the Danish Radio Concert House (Copenhagen, Denmark, 2002–09); the City Hall in Montpellier (France, 2003–11); the Doha Tower (Qatar, 2007–11, see p. 118); Jane's Carousel, Brooklyn Bridge Park (Brooklyn, New York, USA, 2011); "Las Boas" and "Patio Blanco" apartment buildings in Ibiza (Spain, 2006–12); and the Renaissance Barcelona Fira Hotel (Barcelona, Spain, 2008–12, see p. 374). Current work includes the new Philharmonic Hall in Paris (France, 2007–); the Louvre Abu Dhabi (UAE, 2007–); the Tour de Verre in New York (New York, USA, 2007–); and the National Museum of Qatar (Doha, Qatar, 2008–). Jean Nouvel is the architect in charge of the coordination of the Seguin Island urban renewal project in Boulogne-Billancourt (Paris, France, 2009–).

OMA → pp. 114, 136

OMA
Heer Bokelweg 149
3032 AD Rotterdam
The Netherlands

Tel: +31 10 243 82 00
Fax: +31 10 243 82 02
E-mail: office@oma.com
Web: www.oma.com

REM KOOLHAAS created the Office for Metropolitan Architecture in 1975, together with Elia and Zoe Zenghelis and Madelon Vriesendorp. Born in Rotterdam in 1944, Koolhaas worked as a journalist for the *Haagse Post* and as a screenwriter, before studying at the Architectural Association in London. He became well known after the 1978 publication of his book Delirious New York. OMA is currently led by 10 Partners: Rem Koolhaas, Ellen van Loon, Reinier de Graaf, Shohei Shigematsu, Iyad Alsaka, David Gianotten, Chris van Duijn, Ippolito Pestellini Laparelli, Jason Long, and Michael Kokora. The work of Rem Koolhaas and OMA has won several international awards including the Pritzker Prize (2000); the Praemium Imperiale (Japan, 2003); the RIBA Gold Medal (UK, 2004); the Mies van der Rohe—European Union Prize for Contemporary Architecture (2005);

and the Golden Lion Award for Lifetime Achievement at the 12th International Architecture Exhibition—La Biennale di Venezia (2010). OMA's recent projects include the Netherlands Embassy in Berlin (Germany, 2003); the 1850-seat Casa da Música (Porto, Portugal, 2005); Milstein Hall, an extension to the Architecture, Art, and Planning School at Cornell University (New York, USA, 2009–11); New Court, a new headquarters for Rothschild Bank (London, UK, 2011); a Maggie's Center, a cancer care center (Glasgow, UK, 2011); design of the 575 000-square-meter Headquarters and Cultural Center for China Central Television (CCTV, Beijing, China, 2005–12); the Shenzhen Stock Exchange (Shenzhen, China, 2008–13, see p. 136); De Rotterdam (Rotterdam, the Netherlands, 2009–13, see p. 114); and the G-Star Headquarters (Amsterdam, the Netherlands, 2014).

OOS → p. 100

OOS AG
Hard Str. 245
8005 Zurich
Switzerland

Tel: +41 435 00 50 05
E-mail: info@oos.com
Web: www.oos.com

CHRISTOPH KELLENBERGER was born in Zurich, Switzerland, in 1974. He received his architecture degree from the Winterthur Technikum (1994–98). He founded OOS with ANDREAS DERRER, who was born in Uster, Switzerland, in 1974 and also received his architecture degree from the Winterthur Technikum (1994–99). JAN GLOECKNER and GONÇALO MANTEIGAS joined the firm as Partners in 2014. Work of the firm includes interiors of MMP Zurich (Zurich, 2012); Claudia House of Sounds (Winterthur, 2012); Dentalclub I and II (Luzern/Steinhausen, 2013); Wüest & Partner Office (Zurich, 2013); Schlossgut Bachtobel (Weinfelden, 2013); and Villa Kabru/Casa Brasil III (Itacaré, Bahia, Brazil, 2013, see p. 100), all in Switzerland unless stated otherwise.

JOHN PAWSON → p. 318

John Pawson
Unit B
70–78 York Way
London N1 9AG, UK

Tel: +44 20 78 37 29 29
Fax: +44 20 78 37 49 49
E-mail: email@johnpawson.co.uk
Web: www.johnpawson.com

Born in Halifax in central England in 1949, JOHN PAWSON worked in his family's textile mill before going to Japan for four years. On his return, he studied at the Architectural Association in London and set up his own firm in 1981. Pawson may be best known to the general public because of his 1996 book *Minimum*. Some of his more recent work includes Lansdowne Lodge Apartments (London, UK, 2003); Hotel Puerta America in Madrid (Spain, 2005); the Tetsuka House (Tokyo, Japan, 2003–06); Calvin Klein Apartment (New York, USA, 2006); the Sackler Crossing in the Royal Botanic Gardens (Kew, London, UK, 2006); work and renovation of a wing of the Abbey of Our Lady of Nový Dvůr (Czech Republic, 2004; Phase 2, 2009); the Martyrs Pavilion, St. Edward's School (Oxford, UK, 2009); a church renovation concerning the lateral sacristy and chapels (Abbey of Our Lady of Sept-Fons, Burgundy, France, 2009); and a number of apartments in New York (Schrager Penthouse; 50 Gramercy Park North; Hoppe Apartment, etc., 2009). Recent work includes the refurbishment of the St. Moritz Church (Augsburg, Germany, 2011–13, see p. 318); and renovation and conversion into the Design Museum of the former Commonwealth Institute (London, UK, 2015).

PERKINS+WILL → p.466

Perkins+Will
330 N Wabash Avenue, Suite 3600
Chicago, IL 60611, USA

Tel: +1 312 755 0770
Fax: +1 312 755 0775
E-mail: media@perkinswill.com
Web: www.perkinswill.com

RALPH E. JOHNSON was born in Chicago in 1948, and received his B.Arch from the University of Illinois and his M.Arch from Harvard University. He began his career in the office of Stanley Tigerman and joined Perkins+Will in 1976, where he currently serves as its Global Design Director and is a member of the Board of Directors. As well as the Universidade Agostinho Neto (Luanda, Angola, 2002–11, see p. 466), recent Perkins+Will projects include the Shanghai Nature Museum (Shanghai, China, 2014); University Center for Case Western Reserve University (Cleveland, Ohio, USA, 2014); and the Visitor Center for Northwestern University (Evanston, Illinois, USA, 2014). Ongoing work includes the Massachusetts Institute of Technology (MIT) Mixed-Use Lab Development (Cambridge, Massachusetts, USA); the Women and Children's Wellness Center (Nairobi, Kenya); and a research laboratory and athletics center for Northwestern University (respectively in Chicago and Evanston, Illinois, USA).

PEZO VON ELLRICHSHAUSEN
→ pp.86, 176

Pezo von Ellrichshausen
Nonguen 776, 403000 Concepción
Chile

Tel: +56 41 221 0281
E-mail: info@pezo.cl
Web: www.pezo.cl

Pezo von Ellrichshausen was founded in Buenos Aires in 2002 by Mauricio Pezo and Sofía von Ellrichshausen. MAURICIO PEZO was born in Chile in 1973 and completed his M.Arch degree at the Catholic University of Chile (Santiago, 1998). He graduated from the University of Bío-Bío (Concepción, 1999). SOFÍA VON ELLRICHSHAUSEN was born in Argentina in 1976. She holds a degree in Architecture from the University of Buenos Aires (Buenos Aires, 2002). They teach regularly in Chile and have been Visiting Professors at the University of Texas at Austin, and at Cornell University in New York. They were awarded the MCHAP Prize for Emerging Architecture by the IIT (Chicago, 2014), the Rice Design Alliance Prize (Houston, 2012), the V Iberoamerican Architecture Biennial Award (Montevideo, 2006) and the XV Chilean Architecture Biennial Award (Santiago, 2006). Some of their more recent work includes Cien House (Concepción, Chile, 2009–11); Mine Pavilion (Denver, USA, 2013); Gago House (San Pedro, Chile, 2013); and the two works published here: the Solo House (Cretas, Spain, 2013, see p. 86) and the "Blue Pavilion" (London, UK, 2014, see p. 176).

RENZO PIANO → p.236

Renzo Piano Building Workshop
Via P. Paolo Rubens 29
16158 Genoa, Italy

Tel: +39 01 06 17 11
Fax: +39 01 06 17 13 50
E-mail: italy@rpbw.com
Web: www.rpbw.com

RENZO PIANO was born in 1937 in Genoa, Italy. He studied at the University of Florence and at Milan's Polytechnic Institute (1964). He formed his own practice (Studio Piano) in 1965, associated with Richard Rogers (Piano & Rogers, 1971–78)—completing the Pompidou Center in Paris in 1977—and then worked with Peter Rice (Piano & Rice Associates, 1978–80), before creating the Renzo Piano Building Workshop in 1981 in Genoa and Paris. Piano received the RIBA Gold Medal in 1989. Built work after 2000 includes Maison Hermès (Tokyo, Japan, 1998–2001); Rome Auditorium (Italy, 1994–2002); conversion of the Lingotto Factory Complex (Turin, Italy, 1983–2003); the Padre Pio Pilgrimage Church (San Giovanni Rotondo, Foggia, Italy, 1991–2004); the Woodruff Arts Center Expansion (Atlanta, Georgia, USA, 1999–2005); Renovation and Expansion of the Morgan Library (New York, New York, USA, 2000–06); and the New York Times Building (New York, New York, USA, 2005–07). More recently completed work includes the Broad Contemporary Art Museum (Phase 1 of the LACMA expansion, Los Angeles, California, USA, 2003–08); California Academy of Sciences (San Francisco, California, USA, 2008); the Modern Wing of the Art Institute of Chicago (Chicago, Illinois, USA, 2005–09); the Resnick Pavilion (Phase 2 of the LACMA expansion, Los Angeles, USA, 2006–10); the Ronchamp Gatehouse and Monastery (France, 2006–11); the London Bridge Tower (London, UK, 2009–12); the Tjuvholmen Icon Complex (Oslo, Norway, 2009–12); the Kimbell Art Museum Expansion (Fort Worth, Texas, USA, 2010–13, see p. 236); and the renovation and expansion of Harvard Art Museum (Boston, USA, 2010–14). Ongoing work includes the new Whitney Museum at Gansevoort (New York, New York, USA 2007–); the Stavros Niarchos Foundation Cultural Center (Athens, Greece, 2008–); Valletta City Gate (Valletta, Malta, 2008–); and the Botín Art Center (Santander, Spain, 2010–).

CHRISTIAN DE PORTZAMPARC
→ pp.82, 190

Atelier Christian de Portzamparc—
AECDP, 1 Rue de l'Aude
75014 Paris, France

Tel: +33 1 40 64 80 00
Fax: +33 1 43 27 74 79
E-mail: studio@chdeportzamparc.com
Web: www.chdeportzamparc.com

CHRISTIAN DE PORTZAMPARC was born in Casablanca, Morocco, in 1944. He studied at the École des Beaux-Arts, Paris (1962–60), and created his own firm in 1980. He was awarded the 1994 Pritzker Prize. Built projects include the Water Tower (Marne-la-Vallée, 1971–74); Hautes Formes public housing (Paris, 1975–79); an extension for the Bourdelle Museum (Paris, 1988–92); housing, Nexus World (Fukuoka, Japan, 1989–92); a housing complex at the ZAC Bercy (Paris, 1991–94); Cité de la Musique (Paris, 1985–95); and the Crédit Lyonnais Tower (Euralille, Lille, 1992–95). Other works include Grasse Courthouse (Grasse, 1993–97); the LVMH Tower on 57th Street in New York (New York, USA, 1996–99); the extension of the Palais des Congrès in Paris (1996–99); the French Embassy in Berlin (Germany, 1997–2003); the Philarmonic Concert Hall in Luxembourg (Luxembourg, 1997–2005); and the headquarters of *Le Monde* in Paris (2001–05). More recently he has completed the Hergé Museum (Louvains la Neuve, Belgium, 2001–09); Rhone-Alpes County Council Hall (Lyon, 2006–11); Chateau Cheval Blanc Winery (Saint Emilion, 2006–11); Cidade das Artes (Rio de Janeiro, Brazil, 2004–13, see p. 190); and One57 (New York, New York, USA, 2010–14, see p. 82), all in France unless stated otherwise.

RAAAF / ATELIER DE LYON

→ p.180

RAAAF (Rietveld Architecture-Art-Affordances), Westerdok 744
1013 BV Amsterdam, The Netherlands

Tel: +31 20 776 82 73
E-mail: info@raaaf.nl
Web: www.raaaf.com

Atelier de Lyon, Zuiderzeeweg 31
1095 KZ Amsterdam, The Netherlands

E-mail: delyon@xs4all.nl
Web: www.delyon.nl

RONALD RIETVELD was born in 1972, in Gorinchem, the Netherlands. He graduated from the Academy of Architecture in Amsterdam (2003) and won a Prix de Rome in 2006. After that he founded RAAAF (Rietveld Architecture-Art-Affordances) together with his brother ERIK RIETVELD, born in 1969, also in Gorinchem. The studio operates "at the crossroads of architecture, art, and science." RAAAF was elected Dutch Architect of the Year 2013 and has shown installations at international exhibitions at the Museum Boijmans van Beuningen (Rotterdam), Centraal Museum (Utrecht), and was curator of the Dutch Pavilion at the 12th Architecture Biennale of Venice in 2010 (Vacant NL). The project published here, Bunker 599 (Diefdijklinie, the Netherlands, 2010, see p. 180), was carried out in collaboration with the Atelier de Lyon. The Atelier de Lyon was created by the artist ERICK DE LYON, whose work is based on his observations of the Dutch landscape.

TODD SAUNDERS → p.354

Saunders Architecture
Vestre Torggate 22
5015 Bergen, Norway

Tel: +47 55 36 85 06
E-mail: post@saunders.no
Web: www.saunders.no

TODD SAUNDERS was born in 1969 in Gander, Newfoundland (Canada). He obtained his M.Arch from McGill University (Montreal, Canada, 1993–95) and a Bachelor of Environmental Planning from the Nova Scotia College of Art and Design (1988–92). He has worked in Austria, Germany, Russia, and Norway (since 1996). He is a Guest Professor at Cornell University and teaches part-time at the Bergen School of Architecture. His work includes the Aurland Lookout (with Tommie Wilhelmsen, Aurland, 2006); Villa Storingavika (Bergen, 2004–07); Villa G (Hjellestad, Bergen, 2007–09); Sogn og Fjordane Summer Cabin (Rysjedalsvika, 2007–10); and Solberg Tower and Park (Sarpsborg, Østfold, 2010), all in Norway. He is currently realizing the Fogo Island Studios, four of which have been completed out of a program of six (Fogo Island, Newfoundland, Canada, 2010–11), and has also completed the Fogo Island Inn (2010–13, see p. 354) in the same location.

SCHNEIDER+SCHUMACHER

→ p.310

schneider+schumacher, Poststr. 20A
60329 Frankfurt, Germany

Tel: +49 69 25 62 62 62
Fax: +49 69 25 62 62 99
E-mail: office@schneider-schumacher.de
Web: www.schneider-schumacher.de

TILL SCHNEIDER was born in Koblenz, Germany, in 1959. He studied at the Kaiserslautern University and TH Darmstadt (1979–86) and did postgraduate studies with Peter Cook at the Städelschule Frankfurt. He cofounded schneider+schumacher in Frankfurt in 1988. MICHAEL SCHUMACHER was born in 1959 in Krefeld, Germany. He also studied at the Kaiserslautern University (1978–85) and did postgraduate work with Peter Cook in Frankfurt (1986), before forming his partnership with Till Schneider. He worked one year in the office of Norman Foster (London, 1987). Their work includes the Info-Box (Potsdamerplatz, Berlin, 1995); Braun Office Building (Kronberg, 2000); Soviet Special Camp Museum (Sachsenhausen, 2001); Erco Automated Warehouse (Lüdenscheid, 2001); Fronius Research and Development Center (A-Thalheim, 2011); Silvertower (Frankfurt, 2011); Städel Museum (Frankfurt, 2012); Siegerland Highway Church (Wilnsdorf, 2012–13, see p. 310); FAIR Accelerator Facility (Darmstadt); and and Teda School (Tianjin, China, 2016), all in Germany unless stated otherwise.

EDUARDO SOUTO DE MOURA

→ p.370

Souto Moura Arquitectos Lda
Rua do Aleixo 53, 1ºA
4150–043 Porto, Portugal

Tel: +351 226 18 75 47
Fax: +351 226 10 80 92
E-mail: geral@soutomoura.pt

EDUARDO SOUTO DE MOURA was born in Porto, Portugal, in 1952. He graduated from the School of Architecture of Porto (ESBAP) in 1980. He was an Assistant Professor at the Faculty of Architecture in Porto (FAUP) from 1981 to 1991. He worked in the office of Álvaro Siza from 1974 to 1979 and created his own office the following year. He was awarded the Pritzker Prize in 2011. His work includes row houses in Rua Lugarinho (Porto, 1996); the renovation of the Municipal Market in Braga (1997); the Silo Norte Shopping building (Matosinhos, 1998); a house and wine cellar (Valladolid, Spain, 1999); and the project for the Portuguese Pavilion,

Expo Hannover (with Álvaro Siza, 1999). Since 2000, his work includes the conversion of the building of the Carvoeira da Foz (Porto); two houses at Ponte de Lima (2002); and the Braga Stadium (2004). He was coauthor of the Serpentine Gallery Summer Pavilion 2005 in London (UK) with Álvaro Siza and he completed the Bragança Contemporary Art Museum (Bragança) in 2008. More recently he has worked on a winery (Valpaços, 2010); the Berge du Lac housing complex in Bordeaux (France, 2011); and the Multipurpose Pavilion (Viana do Castelo, 2009–13, see p. 370), all in Portugal unless indicated otherwise.

TACOA → p. 96

Tacoa Arquitetos Associados
Avenida Ipiranga 344 cj 312C
São Paulo, SP 01046–000, Brazil

Tel: +55 11 3159 3045
E-mail: tacoa@tacoa.com.br
Web: www.tacoa.com.br

RODRIGO CERVIÑO LOPEZ was born in São Paulo in 1972. FERNANDO FALCON was born in São Paulo in 1978. They both graduated from the FAU-USP, and they have been the Principals of Tacoa Arquitetos Associados since 2005. Their work includes the Adriana Varejão Gallery (Inhotim, Brumadinho, 2005); Plot 40 House (Patrimonio do Carmo, São Roque, 2006); Galpão Fortes Vilaÿa (São Paulo, 2007); Herchcovitch;Alexandre Store (Fashion Mall, Rio de Janeiro, 2009); Galeria Luisa Strina,(São Paulo, 2010); 7 Molinos JK Restaurant, Shopping JK (São Paulo, 2012); the PIVÔ Cultural Center at Edifício Copan (São Paulo, 2013); and Vila Aspicuelta (São Paulo, 2012–13, see p. 96), all in Brazil. They are currently working on housing at Rua Araioses (São Paulo); and a commercial building on Rua Mourato Coelho (São Paulo).

IPPEI TAKAHASHI → p. 452

Takahashi Ippei Office
7F, 2–5–5 Takashima,
Nishi, 220–0011 Yokohama
Japan

Tel: +81 45 441 3516
Fax: +81 50 3737 3162
E-mail: office@takahashiippei.com
Web: www.takahashiippei.com

IPPEI TAKAHASHI was born in 1977 in Tokyo. He graduated from Tohoku University in Sendai in 2000. He completed a Master's degree at the Yokohama National University in 2002, and the same year went to work in the Office of Ryue Nishizawa in Tokyo. While there, he notably participated in the Moriyama House (Tokyo, 2002–05) and the Towada Art Center (Aomori, 2005-08). In 2009, Takahashi created his own firm in Yokohama. His work includes House in N (Tokyo, 2010); Forest Path City (Japan, urban design scheme subsequent to the March 2011 Tohoku Earthquake); the Shichigahama Tohyama Nursery (Miyagi, 2012–13, see p. 452); Casa O (Tokyo, 2013–14); LRT Station and Plaza (Okayama, 2010–); and Sendai New Town project (Sendai, supervising designer, 2011–), all in Japan.

THAM & VIDEGÅRD → p. 78

Tham & Videgård Arkitekter
Blekingegatan 46, 116 62 Stockholm
Sweden

Tel: +46 8 702 00 46
E-mail: info@tvark.se
Web: www.tvark.se

Tham & Videgård was created in 1999 in Stockholm. It is still directed by its cofounders and chief architects BOLLE THAM (born in 1970) and MARTIN VIDEGÅRD (born in 1968). Their work includes the Kalmar Museum of Art (Kalmar, 2004–08); Summer House, Söderöra Island (Stockholm Archipelago, 2007–08); the new Moderna Museet Malmö, the Swedish Museum of Modern Art (Malmö, 2009); Tellus Nursery School (Telefonplan, Stockholm, 2009–10); a tree-house hotel room called Mirrorcube (Harads, 2009–10); a structure for an Electron Microscope/Angströmhouse at the Department of Physics, Chemistry, and Biology at Linköping University (2011); and the Lagnö Summer House (Lagnö, 2012, see p. 78), all in Sweden. They are currently working on the new School of Architecture at the Royal Institute of Technology (Valhallavägen, Stockholm, 2007–2015).

TRIPTYQUE → p. 128

Triptyque
Avenida Europa 342, São Paulo
SP 01447-010, Brazil

Tel: +55 11 3081 3565
E-mail: triptyque@triptyque.com
Web: www.triptyque.com

GREGORY BOUSQUET was born in 1973 in Evry, France. He received his degree as an architect from the École d'architecture Paris-la Seine (1991–97), and further DEA degrees from the École d'architecture Paris-Villemin and Paris IV (Sorbonne, in philosophy, 1998). He worked with the firm Jumeau & Paillard (Paris, 1999), before creating Triptyque in São Paulo in 2002 and in Paris in 2008. CAROLINA BUENO was born in São Paulo, Brazil, in 1974. She received a DEFA degree from the École d'architecture Paris-la Seine (1993–95) and her DPLG from the same institution (1998–2000), as well as a Landscape Certificate from the Brazilian Institute (BRAP) in 2005. She was also a founding Partner of Triptyque. OLIVIER RAFFAELLI, born in 1973 in Neuilly-sur-Seine, France, also received his DPGL at the École d'architecture Paris-la Seine (1991–97), as did GUILLAUME SIBAUD, born in 1973 in Saint-Julien-les-Villas, France. Both Raffaelli and Sibaud were also founding Partners of the firm. Their work includes Sonique (São Paulo, Brazil, 2009); a médiathèque (Osny, France, 2010–12); an office building for INPI in Courbevoie (France, 2012); a commercial building and a residential building in São Paulo (Brazil, 2013); the Oscar Freire building (São Paulo, Brazil, 2013, see p. 128); Groenlandia building (São Paulo, Brazil, 2013); and the Red Bull Station, a cultural center (São Paulo, Brazil, 2013). Among ongoing projects, the Osny Multimedia Library (Paris, France, 2015).

VALODE & PISTRE → p. 350

Valode & Pistre
115 Rue du Bac
75007 Paris, France

Tel: +33 1 53 63 22 00
E-mail: info@v-p.com
Web: www.v-p.com

DENIS VALODE was born in 1946. He received his architecture degree in 1969 from the École des Beaux-Arts in Paris and taught there from 1970 to 1985. JEAN PISTRE was born in 1951 and also studied architecture at the École des Beaux-Arts in Paris, graduating in 1974. The two men first worked together in 1977 and created Valode & Pistre in

1980. Today the office employs up to 200 people and provides interior, architectural, and urban design, as well as engineering services. Their work includes the renovation of 19th-century warehouses in the Bercy district into a modern commercial area (Paris, 1998–2001); the Cap Gemini Ernst & Young campus in Gouvieux (2002); Opus 12 office tower renovation at La Défense (Paris, 2002); and master plan and buildings for the Renault Technocentre in Guyancourt near Paris (2003). More recent work includes the T1 Tower, GDF Suez Headquarters (La Défense, Paris, 2009); Grand Stade de Lille (Lille, 2012); Shenyang Cultural City (Shenyang, China, 2013); and the Beirut Souks Entertainment Center (Beirut, Lebanon, 2010–14, see p. 350), all in France unless otherwise indicated. Ongoing work includes a hospital in Shenzhen (China, 2015);

and the Skolokovo Technopark (Moscow, Russia, 2017).

WANG SHU → p. 458

Wang Shu
Amateur Architecture Studio
1D–200, 218 Nanshan Road
Hangzhou 310002, China

Tel/Fax: +86 571 8716 4708
E-mail: wangshu@caa.edu.cn
Web: www.chinese-architects.com/amateur.html

WANG SHU was born in Ürümqi, China, in 1963. He founded the Amateur Architecture Studio in Hangzhou, China (1997). Since 2007, he has been the head of the Architecture School at the China Academy of Art in Hangzhou. Wang Shu won the Pritzker Prize in 2012. His major built works include the Ningbo Art Museum (Ningbo, 2001–05); Ceramic House (Jinhua, 2003–06); the "Tile Garden," Chinese Pavilion, 10th Venice Architecture Biennale (Venice, Italy, 2006); Vertical Housing (Hangzhou, 2002–07); the New Academy Campus of the China Academy of Art (Hangzhou, 2002–07); Ningbo History Museum (Ningbo, 2003–08); Imperial Street Museum (Hangzhou, Zhejiang, 2009); the 2010 Shanghai Expo, Ningbo Tengtou Pavilion (2010, Shanghai); and Tiles Hill (Hangzhou, 2011–13, see p. 458). Current work includes the City Cultural Center of Jinghua (Jinghua, 2010–); Ninghai "Shi Li Hong Zhuang" Traditional Dowry Museum (Ninghai, 2010–); Contemporary Art Museum in a Dock (Zhoushan, 2010–); and the Buddhist Institute Library of Hangzhou (Hangzhou, 2011–), all in China unless stated otherwise.

INDEX

0

3XN   158, 386, 477

A

B

C

China

D

E

F

CREDITS

IMPRINT

PROJECT MANAGEMENT
Florian Kobler and Inga Hallsson, Berlin

COLLABORATION
Harriet Graham, Turin

PRODUCTION
Frauke Peters, Cologne

DESIGN
Benjamin Wolbergs, Berlin

© VG Bild-Kunst
Bonn 2015, for the works of Erick de Lyon, Christian de Portzamparc, Dominique Jakob, Anish Kapoor, Rem Koolhaas, Brendan Macfarlane, Jean Nouvel

© 2015 TASCHEN GmbH
Hohenzollernring 53
D–50672 Cologne
www.taschen.com

Printed in China
ISBN 978–3–8365–5221–9

To stay informed about TASCHEN and our upcoming titles, please subscribe to our free magazine at www.taschen.com/magazine, follow us on Twitter and Facebook, or e-mail your questions to contact@taschen.com.

EACH AND EVERY TASCHEN BOOK PLANTS A SEED!
TASCHEN is a carbon neutral publisher. Each year, we offset our annual carbon emissions with carbon credits at the Instituto Terra, a reforestation program in Minas Gerais, Brazil, founded by Lélia and Sebastião Salgado. To find out more about this ecological partnership, please check: www.taschen.com/zerocarbon
Inspiration: unlimited. Carbon footprint: zero.

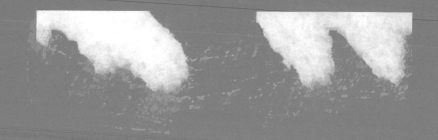

WITHDRAWN FROM STOCK